John Powell, S.J.

Happiness Is an Inside Job

MW006.3942z-7

W0008217

TABOR®
PUBLISHING

Allen, Texas

Cover design: Karen McDonald and Tricia Legault

Book design: Cheryl Carrington

Calligraphy: Bob Niles

Copyright © 1989 by John Powell

All rights reserved. No part of this book shall be reproduced or trans-
mitted in any form or by any means, electronic or mechanical, including photocopying, recording, or by any information or retrieval system,
without written permission from the Publisher.

Send all inquiries to:
Tabor Publishing
One DLM Park
Allen, Texas 75002

Printed in the United States of America

ISBN 1-55924-005-9

    3 4 5   93 92 91 90

Contents

Happiness is a natural condition.

I would like to begin with an assumption that I think you will want to examine carefully. You may want to disagree. In any case, in these pages I am assuming that the natural condition of human beings is to be happy. Something in me is sure that all of us were created to be happy. I believe that God made us to be happy in this world and forever in the next. And so, as I see it, this follows logically: If a person is chronically unhappy, there is something wrong. Something is missing. Obviously, it may not be that person's fault or choice. Still, I would maintain, something is missing. Anyway, please be patient with me as I try to explain my thinking in the pages that follow.

The Inborn Desire — A History of Frustration

I believe that every one of us experiences a stubborn, inborn desire to be happy. Unfortunately, all of us have at times experienced some frustration of this desire. Our dreams of happiness have been disappointed. I am sure that you can remember, as I do, building up an anticipation only to watch it fall apart. We dreamed, for example, that if only there was a "bicycle under the

Christmas tree," life would be forever glorious. Then one Christmas morning, a shiny new bike did appear under the Christmas tree. We were ecstatic. But in the days that followed, the paint began to chip off, the fenders got dented, the axles started squeaking. The dream had slowly, almost painlessly, died. But by this time we had begun another dream anyway. One by one they all seemed to have meteoric moments and then die. Our hopes for *lasting* happiness got lost somewhere along the way.

Expectations and Happiness

Of course, expectations have a lot to do with our happiness. It is one of those life lessons that is hardest to learn. To the extent that we think our happiness will come from outside things or even other persons, our dreams are destined for death. The true formula is, $H = IJ$. Happiness is an inside job.

Most of us are hopeless romantics. And sadly, romantic hope does not die easily. We continue to dream our unreal dreams. We glorify reality with Technicolor expectations. We build castles in the sky. We keep thinking of life and happiness as a combination lock. Once we learn the right combination, we will have it made. But frustration will always overtake us as long as we put our happiness in the promise of things or in the hands of other humans.

A few years ago a divorce lawyer submitted the opinion that most divorces result from romanticized expectations. Jack thinks that being married to Jill will be utter bliss. He calls her "Angel" and "Sweetie." She is all he will ever need. He sings her the romantic lyrics of love songs. Then, shortly after the wedding bells have become an echo, the truth sets in: There are unpleasant moods, weight gains, burned dinners, hair curlers, occasional bad breath and body odors. He silently wonders how he ever got into this. He secretly thinks that she has deceived him. He had gambled his happiness on "Angel Face" and has apparently lost.

On the other side, before marriage Jill's heart beats a little faster whenever she thinks of Jack. It will be such heaven to be married to him. "Just Jackie and me and baby make three . . . in my Blue Heaven." Then there are cigarette ashes, his addiction to sports events on television, minor but painful insensitivities. Clothes are left lying only in chronological order. Her knight in shining armor has turned out to be a "one-man slum." The top of the toothpaste tube is missing. The doorknob he promised to fix still comes off in her hand. Jill cries a lot and starts looking up "marriage counselors" in the yellow pages. Jack carried her off gallantly into the sunset. From then on it was all darkness.

Fifty percent of all marriages end in divorce. Sixty-five percent of all second marriages end in the same traumatic sadness. Disillusion always seems to follow when we expect someone or something else to make us happy. Such expectations are a parade that always gets rained on. The place called "Camelot" and the person called "Right" just don't exist. The anticipations always seem ecstatic, but they are soon swallowed up in the darkness and disappointment of night. Our mistake begins when we expect things and other people to assume responsibility for our happiness. I once saw a cartoon of a huge woman standing over her diminutive, seated husband, demanding, "Make me happy!" It was a cartoon. It was meant for laughter. It was a distortion of reality. That's why it was funny. No one can make us truly happy or truly unhappy.

The Sad Statistics

I am assuming that we are all capable of the "habit of happiness." But the philosopher Thoreau once said that most of us "lead lives of quiet desperation." Thoreau thought that we have given up all hope of true and lasting happiness. The contemporary evidence is overwhelming. It would seem that Thoreau is right. There are growing divorce rates, child- and spouse-abuse epidemics, increased incidence of chemical dependency on alcohol and other drugs. There is the explosion of teenage pregnancies. Gangs prowl our streets. Police patrol the corridors of our high schools. Prisons are bulging. International war clouds are always gathering. Many people think that all this explains our national unhappiness.

Even the air we breathe is certified as polluted. The rain that waters our crops is "acid rain." The food we eat allegedly contains many cancer-causing agents. There is the nightmare of AIDS, which is predicted to claim millions of lives. No one, it is said, can take in this whole scene without some risk of depression. In other words, if you don't feel bad, you apparently haven't been paying attention. Or as Walter Cronkite once put it, "If you think things seem to be going well, you had better have your television set repaired."

It is not surprising that the World Health Organization has singled out *depression* as the world's most widespread disease. One-third of all Americans wake up depressed every day. Professionals estimate that only 10 to 15 percent of Americans think of themselves as truly happy. The highest rate of suicide among professionals is that of psychiatrists. Apparently not even psychiatry provides the right combination for the locked-in secret of happiness. Consequently, there is much cynicism about happiness. Since the search has been largely unsuccessful for most of us, many have given up. So pop a pill, wander into a chemical haze, eat, drink, and try to look merry. "Life is a struggle," someone has said, "and then you die." For many people the promise and possibility of real happiness is only a cruel hoax. It is the mechanical carrot dangled in front of us to make us run faster and try harder.

Advertised Happiness

For all the disillusion we have experienced with the outside, we never seem to look inside for that which we seek. Maybe Dag Hammarskjöld was right when he said that we are great at exploring outer space but very poor at exploring inner space. Perhaps we have been misled by the tidal wave of advertising that washes over us. We are assured that we will be happy if we buy and use certain products. We will look good, sound good, smell good. We will drive along the highways of life with a happy, reckless abandon. These solicitations of the advertising media would have us believe that happiness is simply the multiplication of pleasures.

So we have bought ourselves into debt, consumed all the happiness-making products. Yet we continue to "lead lives of quiet desperation." We haven't been able to cash in on the promotional promises of happiness. There is a story about a young woman selling perfume. Behind her was a large sign: "THIS PERFUME IS GUARANTEED TO GET YOU A MAN!" It seems that a little old spinster lady approached the counter and cautiously asked the salesgirl, "Is it really guaranteed to get a man?" The salesgirl is said to have replied, "If it were really guaranteed, do you think I would be standing here eight hours a day selling this perfume?"

Is it simply that our eyes for happiness are bigger than our digestive tracts? Is it simply a case of unrealistic expectation? I for one don't think it is that simple. I think we are looking for happiness in all the wrong places. We have pinned our hopes on other people and on objects that simply cannot deliver. To remind myself, I have a sign in the mirror over my sink. It reads: "You are looking at the face of the person who is responsible for your happiness." Every day I believe more and more in what that sign says.

Parent Tapes

One of the reasons many of us confuse the sources of happiness is our so-called *parent tapes*. These are the messages of those who influenced us as infants and children. We came into this world seeking answers. And the answers we got early in life were recorded on the memory machines in our heads. All day long and even when we sleep, these parent tapes are playing inside us.

One of the questions the human heart is always asking is this: "What will make me happy?" Most of the answers we received as children were not recited to us but were acted out for us. We learn by seeing, not by being told verbally. We may have observed our parents worrying, so we learned to worry. We may have heard them arguing about money, so we concluded that money is essential to happiness. We may have sensed in their words, body language, and facial expressions an overdependence on others.

Others can make us happy, we concluded. We may have heard accusations like "You make me so mad." And so we may have concluded that others can also make us mad. They apparently can make us happy or unhappy, mad or glad, secure or afraid. Or we may have picked up the old bromide, "If you've got your health, you've got everything." There was a time when I thought of myself as an independent thinker. But the older I get, the more I realize that these parent tapes are very much a part of me and my life. I have to review and revise constantly.

The Comparison and Competition Traps

One of the tapes that plays constantly in most of us is the "comparison" tape. From the time we were presented to the public, we have been compared to others. "He looks like his father." "She looks like her mother." The usual points of comparison are—

- looks,
- brains,
- behavior, and
- accomplishments.

Of course, there were always others who were better looking, smarter, better behaved, and more accomplished than we. Our parents and teachers may have held them up to us. "Why can't you be like that?" "Why don't you do as well as your brother?" "If you comb your hair down, people won't notice your big forehead. You'll look more presentable." And so most of us have been taught to compare ourselves with others. And all the professionals agree: Comparison is the death of true self-contentment.

The "competition" trap is slightly different. In and out of school, most of us have been pitted against others. And, of course, others were pitted against us. We competed for grades, for athletic distinction, for popularity, for membership in the "in groups." Unfortunately, the results of these early contests and competitions have left lifelong scars in many of us. And yet many of us go on competing. In later life, only the status symbols are changed. We still salivate at the sights and sounds of splendor. Inside us the green head of envy groans, "Oh, if only I looked like that . . ." "If only I could think of all those clever things to say . . ." "If I had an estate like that . . ." "If I made that much money . . ." But we don't even come close, and close only counts in the game of horseshoes. In competition, everyone loses.

My Own Experience and Conclusion

My own life experiences have involved me with people in various walks of life. Many others have shared with me their personal struggles and successes. Over the years of this human involvement, I have made many mental notes about the apparent roads to happiness. In addition to this professional involvement, there is my own personal search for happiness. There are clear memories of my own successes and of my own failures. There are certain "dead ends" that look attractive but lead nowhere. There are hills to be climbed one step at a time. There are "traps" into which we can easily fall.

When I sort through all these memories, I am convinced that happiness is within the reach of everyone. The only problem is that if we reach out, we are going in the wrong direction. Happiness is, and has always been, an inside job.

One other important conclusion is this: Happiness is also a by-product. It is the result of doing something else. Like the elusive butterfly, happiness cannot be directly pursued. All attempts to seek happiness directly are doomed. Almost everything else we can search for and acquire directly: food, shelter, knowledge. Not so with happiness. Happiness is attained by doing "something else."

So what is this something else? After much reflection on my own experiences, I am convinced that this something else can be condensed into ten life tasks or practices. I am sure that others might want to disagree or amend the list of the ten things (the "something else") I am proposing. Please feel free. But these are the ten things that I think a person must do to experience true happiness. The explanation of these ten tasks will be the content of this book. These pages are my love offering to you. My hope is that you will take the book in gentle hands and read it with an open mind.

Final Word

These avenues to human happiness are life tasks. They are not simple things that can be done once and for all time to come. It is not like putting so many coins into a happiness-dispensing machine. Then suddenly out comes the candy bar of happiness! That would be selling snake oil. That would be an impostor promising quick-fix happiness. Life is a process, a gradual growth process. We can accomplish our life tasks only gradually. The path to happiness is a bridge to be crossed, not a corner to be turned.

Because happiness is a by-product, the promise is this: The more we accomplish the ten listed life tasks, the more we will attain a sense of personal peace and satisfaction. The more we look within ourselves and not to other things or persons for our happiness, the more we will experience a sense of meaning and direction in our lives. Remember, it is not a question of all or none. It is rather a question of more and more. To live is to grow, and growth is always gradual.

The Latin word *beatus* means "happy." A beatitude is a challenge and an accomplishment. It promises to confer (indirectly) true happiness upon the person who undertakes the challenge and gradually manages the accomplishment.

These are my "beatitudes."

We must accept ourselves as we are.

We tend to hold on to things, including ideas. *We are reluctant to give up ideas like* who I am. *Yet giving up some old ideas is essential to growing. I must learn how to let go of the static image of who I think I am. If I am to grow, I must get unhooked from my past. I must come to realize that I am the one and only me, a person in process—always and forever learning, changing, growing. The only important reality is* who I am right now. *I am not who I used to be. I am not yet who I will be. And above all I must know this: I am who I am supposed to be, and I am fully equipped to do whatever it is I am supposed to be doing with my life.*

The Signs of Self-acceptance

First and foremost, self-acceptance implies a *joyful* satisfaction in being who I am. Simply being resigned to being who I am is only a "for better or for worse" kind of acceptance. It can be discouraging. If I am to be a happy person, I must learn to be happy about who I am. But this is not a simple matter. You see, all of us have an "unconscious" level of the mind. It is a hiding place or a mental burial ground for those things we don't like to face or can't live with. The unfortunate truth is that we do not bury these "eyesores" dead but alive. They continue to influence us. But we are not aware of them or their continuing influence on all our thoughts, words, and actions.

And so it is not a simple matter to confront myself with the questions: "Do I really accept myself? Do I enjoy being who I am? Do I find meaning and satisfaction in being who I am?" The answers that come forth easily and quickly are not fully trustworthy. However, there are reliable signs, or symptoms, of the truth. These signs of self-acceptance will be apparent in my daily living. I would like to list here ten signs that I think are apparent in those who truly and joyfully accept themselves as they are.

1. *Self-accepting people are happy people.*   Strangely, the first sign of true self-acceptance is happiness itself. It sounds like a vicious circle, doesn't it? Yet people who truly enjoy being who they are always have good company. They are with someone they like twenty-four hours a day. On good days and bad, that familiar, delightful person is always there. Not much can make them unhappy. If others are critical or unloving, those who truly love themselves will really believe that there has been a communication problem. Or failing this, they will be led to assume that the critical or unloving person has a personal problem. They will feel sorry for, not angry at, that person.

2. *Self-accepting people go out to others easily.*   The more we accept ourselves as we are, the more we presume that others will like us too. So anticipating their acceptance, we will like

to be with others. We will walk into a room full of strangers confidently, and introduce ourselves around. We will think of ourselves as gifts to be given through self-disclosure, and of others as gifts to be received, gently and gratefully. However, if we truly love ourselves, we will also enjoy and savor the moments of solitude. It has been truly said that for those who joyfully accept themselves, being alone is a peaceful solitude. For those who do not accept themselves, being alone can mean a painful loneliness. The lonely experience a vacuum and can only look for distractions—a newspaper, a cup of coffee, a blaring radio.

3. *Self-accepting people are always open to being loved and complimented.* If I truly accept and enjoy being myself, I will understand it when others also love me. I will be able to accept love from others graciously and gratefully. I won't have to wrestle with the unspoken regret: "If you really knew me, you wouldn't love me." I will also be able to take in, to interiorize, favorable comments and compliments. I will be comfortable with such compliments. I won't have to be constantly suspicious of the motives of the giver of compliments: "Okay, what's your angle?" "What do you want?" I won't have to moan sadly to myself, "Oh, you can't be serious."

4. *Self-accepting people are empowered to be their "real" selves.* To the extent that I truly and joyfully accept myself as I am, I will have about me an authenticity that can follow only from genuine self-acceptance. In other words, I have to accept myself before I can be myself. I will be real. When my feelings are hurt, I will be able to say an audible "Ouch!" When I love and admire another, I will be honest and open about sharing my love and admiration with that person. I won't be tortured by the possibility of misunderstanding or misinterpretation. I won't be worried about whether my feelings are mutual or not. In a word, I will be free to be me.

This authenticity means that I won't have to carry around with me, as a kind of bag and baggage of life, a set of masks. I will face the honest fact: I don't have to please you, but I do have to be me. What you see is what you get. This is me, the one and only me, an original by God. There are no carbon copies anywhere. Most of us have been putting on a mask or playing a role so long that we don't know where the mask-role ends and the real me begins. But we do have a gut instinct about genuineness. We have a relieving sense of honesty when we have been our true selves.

5. *Self-accepting people accept themselves as they are right now.*   Yesterday's me is history. Tomorrow's me is unknown. Getting unhooked from my past and not living in anticipation of the future is far from simple or easy. But the only real self-acceptance must focus on who I am at this moment. An old humorous verse puts it this way:

> "Your *wasness* doesn't matter
> if your *isness* really am."

What I have been, including all the mistakes I have made, doesn't really matter. What does matter is who I am right now. Self-acceptance of the right-now me is likewise not filled with anticipation of the me I will become. If I love or allow another to love only the potential me, this love is useless, if not destructive. It is not *unconditional,* which is an essential quality of all real love. It says only, "I will love you if you will become . . ." As good old Charlie Brown once put it, "The greatest suffering in life is to have a great potential."

6. *Self-accepting people are able to laugh at themselves, often and easily.*   Taking oneself too seriously is an almost certain sign of insecurity. An old Chinese beatitude has it: "Blessed are they who can laugh at themselves. They shall never cease to be entertained." Being able to admit and laugh at one's own fragility and folly requires an inner security that is born only of self-acceptance. Only when I know that I am essentially good can I admit that I am also limited. I can even laugh when these limitations rise to the surface of life and get recognized by others. "I never promised you a rose garden, did I?"

7. *Self-accepting people have the ability to recognize and attend to their own needs.*   First of all, self-accepting people are in

touch with their own needs—physical, emotional, intellectual, social, and spiritual. And second, it is true that charity in this context begins at home. If I do not love myself, I certainly cannot love anyone else. Trying to ignore one's own needs is a suicide course. I must love my neighbor as myself. However, it is almost a truism that if I truly and genuinely love myself, I will be empowered to love my neighbor, spontaneously and naturally.

Self-accepting people seek to live the kind of balanced life in which their needs are met. They generally get enough rest, relaxation, exercise, and nourishment. They refrain from all excesses and self-destructive habits like overeating, smoking, drunkenness, and the use of drugs. Also, they are able to weigh their own needs in balance with the needs, requests, and demands of others. They are attentive to the needs of others, whom they often help with compassion. However, they can also say no to others without a lingering feeling of regret or guilt. They know their own limitations and needs.

8. *Self-accepting people are self-determining people.*   They take their cues from inside themselves, not from other people. If I truly and joyfully accept myself, I will do what I think is right and appropriate, not what other people may think or say. Self-acceptance is relatively immune to mob psychology or the crowd spirit. It is not afraid to swim upstream when necessary. As Fritz Perls would say, "I did not come into this world to live up to your expectations. And you did not come into the world to live up to mine."

9. *Self-accepting people are in good contact with reality.*   This kind of contact with reality is sometimes more easily explained by describing its opposite. It precludes daydreaming or imagining myself in another life as another person. I deal with myself as I really am, with others as they really are. I do not waste useless energy regretting that we are not otherwise. I enjoy and engage myself with life as it really is. I don't wander off mentally into what "might" have been.

10. *Self-accepting people are assertive.*   The final sign of self-acceptance is what is called assertiveness. As a self-accepting

person, I assert my right to be taken seriously, the right to think my own thoughts and to make my own choices. I enter all relationships only as an equal. I will not be the compulsive underdog or the compulsive helper of the helpless. I will also assert my right to be wrong. Many of us retreat from true assertiveness on the grounds that we might be wrong. We bury our opinions, refuse to make known our preferences. Joyful self-acceptance challenges us to be assertive—to respect ourselves, to express ourselves openly and honestly.

Is Self-acceptance Only Disguised Self-centeredness?

There is an instinct that causes most of us to blush whenever we are told that we must love ourselves. We experience a very real fear of self-centeredness. I don't know if we still speak of "capital sins," but right at the head of the old list was *pride*. The surprising fact of the matter is that self-centeredness, or narcissism, has been shown to result from self-loathing, not self-liking. The self-centered person feels empty and tries to fill this painful void with bragging, competing, triumphing over others, and so forth. In the self-liking person, the civil war of self-acceptance is over. The guns are quiet. The darkness is gone. The pain that magnetized all attention to self has subsided. There is peace at last. There is a new freedom to go out of self to others. Only those who truly and joyfully accept themselves can achieve the self-forgetfulness of loving and caring for others.

It is in this context that Carl Jung, the great psychiatrist, said, "We all know what Jesus said about the way we treat the least of our brothers and sisters. But what if we were to discover that the least, the most needy of these brothers and sisters is *me?*" Very often, good and decent people think that being disappointed with themselves is healthy. What they see as an "angel of light" is really a temptation. "I expected to be better than I am" is a discouraging thought. It is devastating to our realization of the love God has for each of us. While self-disappointment may seem very humble and objective, it in fact undermines the experience of being loved, and it discredits any affirming comments made of me or of my achievements. Self-disappointment will silently rob me of the happiness for which I was created.

As I see it, pride and true humility begin the same way: by realizing and savoring one's own goodness and giftedness. Then virtue and vice part company. Pride claims this goodness and giftedness as personal accomplishment. Pride listens for applause, sniffs for incense. Pride is lonely without recognition and reward. Humility quietly knows that "I have nothing which I was not given." Humility is grateful, not grasping.

The Obstacles to Self-acceptance

Someone has wisely said that before we can seek an adequate solution, we have to define the problem clearly. So we ask, "Why do so many of us have such a hard time with self-acceptance?" I think the answer is that all of us have inferiority complexes. Those who seem not to have such a complex are only pretending.

We came into this world asking questions for which we had no answers. The most obvious question we asked was, "Who am I?" From birth to age five we supposedly got an average of 431 negative messages every day. "Get down from there." "No, you're too small." "Give me that! You'll hurt yourself." "Oh, you've made another mess." "Be quiet, please. I've had a hard day." A friend of mine swears that until he was eight, he thought his name was "Freddy No-No." No doubt this first impression of our inadequacy has stayed with us.

It is also true that the obstacles to self-acceptance are as unique in each of us as our personal histories. The causes and reasons I can't fully enjoy being me are somewhat different from the causes and reasons you can't enjoy being you. And so, in order to define the problem more clearly, let's start with five general categories. Which of the following is most difficult for you to accept about yourself? Which is easiest? As you continue reading, make some mental notes about the way you would rank the following in the order of your personal difficulty. Rank them from the most serious obstacle to self-acceptance to the least serious.

- my body
- my mind
- my mistakes
- my feelings or emotions
- my personality

Do I Accept My Body?

Physical appearance is probably the first and most frequent point of comment and comparison. Consequently, for many of us, it has become a serious obstacle to self-acceptance. Many clinical psychologists believe that physical appearance is the most important factor in most people's self-esteem. Almost all of us would like to change at least one physical feature. We would like to be taller or shorter, have thicker hair or a smaller nose. A test of self-esteem that I once read asked me to stand in front of a full-length mirror. The instructions continued: "Then turn around and around, examining your physical appearance with a critical eye. Then look at yourself in the mirror and ask, 'Do I like being who I am, physically?' " Sometimes, beautiful people are not packaged very beautifully. And so I must ask myself honestly, "How does my packaging affect my self-acceptance?" Anything but an honest answer is a poor place to start.

Most plastic surgeons maintain that when a physical abnormality is corrected in a patient, there is an almost immediate psychological change. The person who looks better becomes more socially outgoing, more pleasant and confident. An orthopedic physician once told me that he asks his older female patients to wear makeup and have their hair done. He makes similar, appropriate suggestions to his male patients. He smiled and added, "It's amazing how an improved appearance raises the self-image and morale of my patients."

Another part of physical self-acceptance concerns our health. Often, strong people do not come equipped with strong bodies.

For genetic or other reasons, many of us have to live with some bodily affliction—weak lungs or weak eyes, spastic colons or nervous stomachs, skin problems, epilepsy or diabetes. We have to be fearless in asking ourselves how these physical disabilities affect our self-acceptance. Again, the only constructive starting point is utter honesty. Only the truth can set us free.

Do I Accept My Mind?

In almost any school or job situation, some emphasis is placed on intelligence. In our personal relationships, there is often an intellectual competition between the partners. Many of us carry inside us painful memories of being embarrassed or laughed at in a classroom or a social situation. Others looked at us almost pityingly or ridiculed our comment, question, or behavior.

So we must ask ourselves if we feel comfortable with the amount and quality of the intelligence we have been given. Am I tempted to compare myself with others on this basis? Am I intimidated by others who seem mentally quicker or more informed than I? My self-esteem and consequently my happiness may be seriously involved with these questions and my answers to them.

Do I Accept My Mistakes?

The human condition is one of weakness. This is why there are erasers on pencils. We are all mistake makers. God has equipped his animals and birds with infallible instincts. We human beings have to learn most things by trial and error. An old sage once said, "Try to learn from the mistakes of others. You won't live long enough to make them all yourself." Most of us take it for granted that if you haven't made a mistake, you have probably never made a discovery. Obviously, the only real mistake is the one from which you have learned nothing. Mistakes are learning experiences. So welcome to the club!

As with most virtues, the spirit of understanding and tolerance begins at home. Somehow most of us have to come to a point of ego-desperation before we can offer ourselves a gentle understanding. We have to hit the proverbial bottom before we can begin to rise again.

So I must ask myself: Where am I? Have I let go of rehashing my "mistake-riddled" past? Have I let go of the feelings of embarrassment about my failures and regrets? Can I honestly and with peace say, "This is the person I used to be, the old me. It is not the person I am now, the new and present me"? Most of us do not realize that we have learned from our past mistakes and that we have outgrown some of our immaturities. Do I realize that the *old me* has taught the *new me* many things?

The trap here is to identify with the dark side of my person and the mistakes of my past. It is to think of myself as I once was. It's something like the person who was fat as a child, but who has become slender as an adult. The important question is, Do I think of myself as fat or thin? Clearly, growth requires change, and change means "letting go." How difficult or easy is this for you? Remember, we have to start with a ruthless honesty or we may never come to the truth. And without the truth there is no growth, no joy.

Do I Accept My Feelings or Emotions?

Mood swings are common to most of us. One moment we may feel "up," the next "down." But some feelings are quarantined out of existence by our early programming. For example, I always found it hard to admit fear because my father insisted that "a man is not afraid of anything or anyone." Some of us feel obliged to repress the emotion of jealousy or feelings of self-satisfaction. Someone has somehow taught us that these emotions are simply not allowed. One valid emotion that is almost universally condemned is self-pity. We have all either heard or made the accusation, "Oh, you're only feeling sorry for yourself."

It seems to be true that we handle emotions according to what we think about them. And so we must ask: Are there emotions active in me that I allow to become an obstacle to joyful self-acceptance? Can I feel fear, hurt, anger, jealousy, resentment, self-satisfaction, or self-pity without getting involved in self-criticism and self-condemnation? Are there feelings I would like to conceal in the hope that they will just go away?

Do I Accept My Personality?

Without going into detail, I think it is safe to assume that there are personality types. These types seem to be partly genetic and partly the result of early programming. Of course, within each personality type, there are healthy and unhealthy individuals. And there is always room for growth. However, the basic type is usually pretty well set in us. Some of us are extroverts, others introverts. Some are born leaders, others are loyal followers. Some are quiet, others talkative. Some of us are funny, others can't even read a joke well. Some are thick-skinned, others very sensitive. But each of us is unique, different from all others. Our very gifts distinguish us. Our limitations define us. From what I know of my basic personality type, am I happy to be me? Does my basic personality seem attractive or regrettable to me?

To better understand my personality, it might help to make a list of the five qualities that describe me best: quiet, plain, diplomatic, funny, verbal, emotional, involved, lonely, joyful, troubled, and so forth. Then I should ask a close but very honest friend to make a similar list of qualities that best describe me, capture my personality. Putting the two lists together should give me a starting point. My personality is me-in-action. Do I like what I see, or am I a disappointment to myself? Would I want to change my personality radically, or am I satisfied with who I am? Would I choose someone like myself for a close friend?

Programming and Self-acceptance

Someone has humorously remarked that the smartest thing a child can do is to make a wise selection of parents. Joyful self-acceptance gets its deepest roots in infancy and childhood. We humans are something like computers. Everything we have ever seen, heard, or experienced remains stored forever in our brains. Now, the average human brain weighs only three pounds, three ounces. But neurologists suggest that if a computer were ever built to store as many messages as the human brain can, that computer would be ten stories tall and would cover the state of Texas. Rudolph Dreikurs, an Adlerian psychiatrist, has suggested that it isn't what was said to us but what we heard (experienced) that counts. And as suggested earlier, what most of us heard and experienced did not always assure us that each of us is a wonderful work of God, destined to grow into the full stature of a magnificent human being.

A woman who teaches in a Montessori preschool once told me a not so surprising story. The school sends out a registration form to the parents of prospective preschoolers. One of the questions asked is this: "Is there anything we should know about your child before the beginning of class?" Some of the parents answer, "Oh, our child is just wonderful. You will really like our child." The teacher explained to me, "We have learned to expect peak performance from these children. They are self-confident, assertive, and always seem to enjoy themselves." Of course, many of the parents write that their children are easily upset, have tantrums, and cry very easily. My Montessori teacher friend shook her head sadly. "They act out their insecurities as predicted. They become the self-fulfilling prophecies of their parents."

It is important to know that we can edit these parent tapes. We can, even as adults, "record over" any demoralizing messages. Of course, we will want to keep those that are healthy and supportive. The human mind is like a garden. If we want flowers to grow there, it has to be weeded. We should each begin this process by making a list of the messages that have been programmed into us. Then we should separate them into two categories: the supportive and healthy as opposed to the demoralizing and unhealthy. We should also make a list of all our special gifts and personal blessings. Soon the flowers will start appearing. We will begin to be more aware of our personal goodness and giftedness. Beauty will gradually replace the ugliness that has held us captive.

The Central Realization:
I Am Who I Am Supposed to Be!

Whatever our religious preference is, this much is certainly true of God and our creation: Your story and mine did not begin with our entrance into this world. From all eternity God has thought about and loved you and me. Oh, God could have made us different. God could have allotted us a different set of gifts, given us a different set of genes. But then you and I would not be who we in fact are. And God wanted you to be you and me to be me, just as we are. There were many other possible worlds that God could have created. But one of the reasons God chose this world as we know it is that you are you and I am I.

It is an old Jewish-Christian tradition that God sends each of us into this world with a special message to deliver, with a special act of love to bestow. Your message and your act of love are entrusted only to you, mine to me. Whether this message is to reach only a few or all the folks in a small town or all the people in the whole world depends totally on God's choice. The only important conviction is that each of us is fully equipped. You have just the right gifts to deliver your message, and I have the carefully selected gifts to deliver mine.

A special piece of God's truth has been put into your hands, and God has asked you to share it with the rest of us. The same is true of me. And just as you are the one and only you, your truth is given to you alone. No one else can tell the world your truth or bestow on others your act of love. Only you have all the requirements to be and do what you are to be and do. Only I have all that is needed to complete the task for which I was sent into this world.

It would be futile and even foolish to compare myself with you. Each of us is unique. There are no carbon copies or clones of either of us. Such a comparison would be the death of joyful self-acceptance. Look at your hand. The fingers are not of equal length. If they were, you could not effectively hold a baseball bat or knitting needles. Just so, some of us are tall and others are short. Some of us have one talent, others have a different gift. You are tailor-made to do your thing. I am made to do mine. And so you are not me, and I am not you. And that is good, very good. We must not only accept but even celebrate our differences. The world treasures originals, and each of us is an original by God.

Processing These Ideas about Self-acceptance

Anyone who has done much public speaking knows that it is very important to ask the audience somehow to process the ideas presented. The same thing is true with the written word. The reader must be asked to do something in order to appropriate the convictions presented. Spoken or written words that just wash over us leave nothing permanent in us or in our lives. However, when we take the time to work through ideas, to compare them to our own experience, they eventually become ours and a part of our lives. And when this happens, we change. So at the end of each of the practices presented in this book, suggestions for your personal processing are included. What you do will prove more motivating and life changing than the words you will read. Your own activity will generate a new enthusiasm in you. Trust me, and please try the following.

1. *Write in a Journal-Notebook.* Note which category of self you find hardest to accept: (*a*) my body, (*b*) my mind, (*c*) my mistakes, (*d*) my feelings or emotions, (*e*) my personality.

Sit and reflect. Explore your inner spaces. Try to describe in writing what you find hardest to accept about yourself—and why.

What would you say to someone else who has your "problem" with self-acceptance?

2. *See Yourself in the Empty Chair Fantasy.* Sit quietly and preferably alone. Assume a comfortable position and close your eyes. Try to relax by inhaling deeply but without straining. Exhale completely. Empty your lungs so that the next inhalation will bring into your lungs a completely fresh supply of oxygen.

While you are breathing this way, try to imagine the whole network of muscles in your body. See your muscles and nerves as stretched and taut rubber bands. Then imagine that those same muscles and nerves are unstretching, relaxing. Feel yourself sinking slowly into peace and tranquillity.

Now imagine an empty chair about ten feet in front of you, facing you. Notice all the details of the chair. What kind of chair is it? What color is it? Does it look comfortable? Is it upholstered? Bring it into sharp focus. Imagine someone you know very well, someone perhaps with whom you work or go to school, a member of your family. See this person coming out from the wings of the stage and sitting in the chair, looking at you. Notice how the person looks at you. Is he or she comfortable with you? As you return the person's glance, you will gradually become aware of a "felt-sense" reaction to that person. All your experiences with this person, the feelings you have had in dealing with this person, and all the judgments you have made about this person—all these will feed into and form a felt-sense reaction. After your reaction becomes quite clear to you, prepare to say one thing to that person. What would you most like to say or ask? Silently say it. Then watch the person get up and leave.

Now a second person you know very well comes and sits in the chair. You become aware of the way this person looks at you, and of your own felt-sense reaction to this person. You notice that it is different from your reaction to the first person. When this is quite clear, you silently say one thing to this second person. Then you watch this person get up from the chair and leave.

The third person to come out from the wings of the stage is you. Your imagined self sits in the chair and looks directly back at you. You notice the look on the face of your imagined self. Slowly but surely you become aware of your felt-sense reaction to yourself. You sense the extent to which you really like or dislike yourself and why. You wonder about things you see in yourself, and you become aware of the reactions on the face and in the body language of your imagined self. You silently speak to yourself. You say whatever is in your heart. Then you watch yourself slowly rise from the chair and leave.

Open your eyes now. And write down your reactions to yourself. How did your imagined self look back at you? Did you like the person you saw? Would you choose such a person for a friend? Did you feel sorry for yourself? Were you pleased with yourself? Did your imagined self look tired or energetic? Did you like your physical appearance? What did you say to yourself? Write down all the essentials.

3. *Compose Two Lists.*   The first is a list of all those things you consider to be your personal assets or blessings: your special qualities, physical endowments, abilities, talents, gifts, and so forth. This will, of course, be an ongoing exercise. In the days and years to come you will find in yourself more and more blessings of giftedness and goodness. So keep writing down what you discover.

On the second list record the personal limitations and regrets that most disturb you. This second list is a kind of housecleaning. True self-acceptance must start with an honest evaluation. We must not be discouraged by our limitations, nor should we attempt to deny them. We do not celebrate our regrets or congratulate ourselves for our neuroses. True self-acceptance means accepting some painful truths about ourselves. We are all limited human beings. Without facing that fact, we will be living in a world of pretense and fantasy. Unless we accept and face our limitations, we will not see clearly the direction of our future development and growth.

It would be helpful to share both lists with a trusted confidant. Having made this inventory of strengths and weaknesses, we will be ready to begin "the first day of the rest of our lives." It will be the beginning of true self-esteem, a lifelong celebration of the "one and only you and me"!

Remember

Each of us is an original by God. There are no carbon copies anywhere.

We must accept full responsibility for our lives.

ccepting full responsibility for all our actions, including our emotional and our behavioral responses to all life situations, is the definitive step toward human maturity. However, the tendency to blame our responses on other persons or things is as old as the human race. Many of us grew up as blamers. We defended our most unacceptable behavior: "You had it coming." "You did the same thing to me." "I'm just giving you a taste of your own medicine." We learned to explain away our failures on the grounds that we did not have the right materials to work with, or we even pleaded that "our stars were not in proper alignment; the moon was not in the right house." The essential sadness is that blamers are not in contact with reality. As a result, they do not get to know themselves. They do not mature. They do not grow. It is a fact of life: Growth begins where blaming ends. *The opposite of this blaming tendency is to accept full responsibility for our lives, to* become an owner, not a blamer. *Owners know that something in them explains their*

*emotional and behavioral responses to life. It is clearly
the definitive step toward human maturity. Responsibility ensures that we will grow up.*

What Is "Full Responsibility"?

Every one of us knows from personal experience that we are not completely free. There are times when our reactions completely escape from the reins of self-control. We cannot turn our emotions on and off as though they were controlled by faucets. There are times when we just cannot be all that we want to be, do what we want to do, or say only those things we want to say. Sometimes our habits hold us captive. They seem unbreakable. Our yesterdays lie heavily upon our todays, and our todays will lie heavily upon our tomorrows. We cry when we know we should be laughing. We overeat or overdrink even when we know that this is not good for us. We pout when we know we should be talking something out. So, what's this about accepting "full responsibility"?

Granted that we are not fully free. We have all been programmed from infancy through childhood. And this programming limits our freedom. Also, we have practiced our habits so long and faithfully. Habits, too, diminish our freedom to choose. And sometimes just plain old human inertia often controls us. With Saint Paul we must admit, "I see the right thing, I intend to do it, and then I do just the opposite. There is another law warring within me."

Clearly, full responsibility does not imply full freedom. In this context, what full responsibility means is this: There is *something in me* that determines my actions and responses to the various stimulations and situations of life. It may be the result of my genes, my programming, or the force of my own habits. But it is *something in me.* I take full responsibility for that. I do what I do, I say what I say, because of something in me. Other persons or situations may *stimulate a response,* but the *nature of that response* will be determined by something in me.

First, let's take a look at the meaning of *full responsibility for all my actions*. One of my favorite illustrations is the well-known story of the late Sydney Harris. Accompanying a friend to a newsstand, Harris noted that the man selling papers was openly sullen and cantankerous. He also noted that his friend was kind and cordial in his dealing with this man. As he walked away with his friend, Harris asked, "Is that fellow always so mean?" "Yes, unfortunately he is," the friend answered. Harris persisted, "And are you always so nice to him?" "Yes, of course," answered the friend. So Harris asked the question that was stirring in him from the beginning: "Why?"

Harris's friend had to think, as though the answer were obvious. "Because," he finally explained, "I don't want him or anyone else to decide how I am going to act. *I decide how I am going to act.* I am an *actor,* not a *reactor."* Sydney Harris walked away, mumbling to himself, "That's one of the most important realizations and accomplishments in life: to be an actor, not a reactor."

Full Responsibility and Transactional Analysis

Eric Berne and Thomas Harris are the two psychiatrists who have originated and popularized what is called Transactional Analysis. They say (perhaps more elaborately) the same thing as the friend of Sydney Harris. The theory of Transactional Analysis tells us that there are three components in all of us: *parent, adult,* and *child.* The *parent* in us is a collection of all the messages and programming recorded in us in the early years of life. The *adult* in us is our own mind and will, which make us capable of thinking for and choosing for ourselves. The *child* in us is the storehouse of all our emotional or feeling responses. The psychiatrists of T.A. maintain that those emotions which were experienced most strongly in the first five years of life tend to be the most strong in us for the rest of our lives.

The T.A. theory is that we can analyze our transactions with others and can tell whether the *parent, adult,* or *child* has been in control. Human maturity, the theory continues, is achieved by keeping the *adult* in charge of making all our decisions. We must hear and edit our parent tapes, and we must fully and freely have our feelings. However, we must never let them make our decisions. We must never let our parent-tape programming or our feelings *decide* how we are going to act. We must think for ourselves and choose to act in a mature way.

So accepting full responsibility does not mean that I am completely free. It does not even imply full and complete control by my *adult*. It does, however, mean that I honestly acknowledge that *something in me* determines and controls all my actions and responses. This something in me may be my parental programming overpowering my mind. It may be an explosion of emotions that deprive me, at least in part, of my freedom. So even when I am a reactor as opposed to an actor, it is still something in me that determines my reaction.

Most of us can remember times when the *parent* or the *child* has prevailed in us. Afterward we knew that the *adult* in us would have acted differently. Maybe we allowed some parental message to keep us silent when we should have spoken up. Maybe we childishly refused to apologize when an apology was in order. The *adult* in us would have spoken up, would have apologized. We recognize the difference. When my *adult* is in charge, I think independently and make rational decisions. I take my cues from within my own self. I do not let others decide how I am going to act. Whatever the case may be, I still have to acknowledge and take full responsibility for the *parent, adult,* and *child* in me. Even when I let the *parent* or the *child* decide how I am going to act, I am still directed by something in me. It is my responsibility.

Full Responsibility and Our Emotions

Now we proceed to a more difficult matter: *full responsibility for our emotions or feelings*. Many of us have grown accustomed to the myth that we are not responsible for our feelings. This may have been true of us when we were infants and even children. We did not have an adult in us to sort through our messages and emotions. In a sense we were at the mercy of those older people around us. As adults it is far from the truth. Emotions may still arise quickly and spontaneously in us. However, as responsible adults we can fully and freely experience them, and then decide how we can express them constructively and maturely. Later, perhaps in a reflective moment, we can trace our spontaneous feelings to their roots. Why did I react that way?

By definition, an *emotion* is a *perception* that results in an overflow into a *physical reaction*. Because an emotion is a perception and a consequent physical reaction to that perception, we could not have emotions if we did not have minds and bodies. For example, if I perceive you as my friend, physically I will have a comfortable and peaceful reaction to you. Emotionally I am glad to see you. However, if I perceive you as an enemy, my physical reaction will be one of fight or flight. My muscles will grow tense and my heartbeat will accelerate. I will be afraid of you and what you might be planning to do or say to me.

While I might not be free to control this emotional reaction, I do know that it is caused by *something in me:* my perception of you. This perception may be right or wrong. It may be colored by other experiences, but it is clearly something in me that directs my emotional response.

This is easily illustrated in a classroom situation. I often put this case to my students: "Imagine that one of you walks out of this classroom angrily. You express disgust with me and my teaching ability. How would I feel?" Usually my students are quick to volunteer: "You would feel angry. You would remind the student that you know his name and have his social security number." Another disagrees: "No, you would feel hurt. You know you try hard to be a good teacher. You would be sad that all your efforts would get such a response." Still another offers the opinion: "No, I think you would feel guilty. You would ask the student to come back and give you another chance. You might even try to apologize." Someone almost always suggests a compassionate response:

"You would feel sorry for the kid. You would reason that no doubt there are other tensions that are getting to him."

By the end of the discussion I have usually collected ten or eleven suggestions about my possible emotional response to such a situation. (I secretly suspect that most of the students are projecting how they would feel.) Anyway, I then suggest that I might well react in any of the ways suggested. Then I add with great emphasis, "But notice this. There really are so many possible reactions, ways I might respond. I'm not sure how I would actually respond. But this much is clear: My emotional reaction would be caused by something in me and not by the student walking out. Such a person can only stimulate *a reaction.* Something in me will determine *the precise emotional reaction* I will have. What I think of myself, how I regard myself as a teacher, the importance I attach to the matter I am presenting—all these things inside me will determine my precise emotional reaction. I must accept full responsibility for this. And this is what I mean by accepting full responsibility for my emotions."

Many of my emotional responses are good. Others tend to be self-destructive. So when I reflect upon my emotional reaction in a given situation, I go back to the perception where it all began. I can question and enlarge upon or even alter that perception. Maybe I should take another look. Maybe you were just trying to be friendly, not to embarrass me. It might be that I perceived myself to be inferior, and instead of admitting that, I might have tried to cover it up with conceit. I know this: If I question and perhaps change my perception, my emotional response will also change.

Owners Versus Blamers

In trying to account for our behavioral and emotional responses, I suppose that we have only two real choices. Either we "own" them or we "blame" them on someone or something else. But this is not a simple choice without consequences. My honesty can put me on the road to maturity, or my rationalizing will remove me from reality. If I own my responses, take responsibility for my emotions and behavior, I will get to know myself. I will grow up. If I try to explain my actions and feelings by shifting responsibility to other persons or situations, I will never get to know my real self. I will stunt my personal growth as long as I persist in this unwillingness to acknowledge my responsibility. Remember: *Growth begins where blaming ends.*

Sometime notice how differently people react to the very same person or situation. Take the case of an obnoxious or offensive person. We might be feeling anger toward this person only to discover that a third party feels sorry for this obnoxious person. It all depends on one's perception. Obviously, if I have perceived that person as deliberately malicious, my emotional response might well be that of anger or resentment. My behavioral response might be sarcasm. But if I see that obnoxious person as hurting or deprived, my reaction will probably be compassionate.

Note that in revising our perceptions or attitudes (practiced or habitual perceptions), we also revise our emotional responses. It is important to remember that a perception is always at the heart of every emotion. It is that perception which will determine the nature and intensity of the emotion. It is probably true that many of my emotions are healthy and happy. However, if my emotional patterns are self-destructive or socially alienating, I may want to look at the perceptions or attitudes that are writing my life script. This is certainly a part of my "full responsibility."

Does Assuming Full Responsibility Really Make Us Happy?

This is a good if not obvious question. My own answer is, "Not automatically nor immediately." I'm sure you have heard that the truth will set you free, but first it may make you a little miserable. Unfortunately, our yesterdays do lie heavily upon our todays. Our habits can be deeply ingrained. Such habits, like "flying off the handle," can temporarily and partially limit our freedom of re-sponse. Saying that "I have a short fuse," or that "I have hot blood," is only blaming. It's really not a matter of my fuse or my blood. It's a matter of habit. Our responses of the past were probably learned from others. Worriers tend to beget worriers. Short fuses tend to run in the same families. However, our own repetition of these responses may have dug deep grooves of habit in us. Eventually, they become automatic reactions. You press this button and you get this response. We become slaves to our habits. We are the "trained animals," and habits are the "hoops" we jump through. We can easily keep responding poorly to given situations, for example, by losing our tempers. But if we allow this to become an irreplaceable habit, we tend to get stuck or arrested at that point of our personal growth. When this happens, we naturally tend to blame other persons or situations for our responses. Once we get trapped in this vicious circle, we get stuck in a place of pain. And we stay there.

However, if we assume the full responsibility described above, we are then free to recognize and revise our responses. And this is certainly the pathway to peace and personal happiness. I can't change the world to suit me, but I can change my response to the world. I can change me. *Happiness is an inside job.*

Owners, Blamers, and Self-knowledge

Ancient wisdom insists that self-knowledge is the pinnacle of wis-dom. Unfortunately, if I blame my actions and feelings on someone or something else, I will learn nothing about myself. The unfortu-nate *blamer* keeps assigning responsibility to other people, other places, or other things: "You made me mad." "This place bores me." "Your test frightened me." "He made me feel so small." The poor blamer keeps repeating supposed facts. It is a classic ego-defense mechanism called projection. Once stuck here, the blamer is removed from reality. There is no possibility of growing up. The magnificence of what might have been is lost until the blamer becomes an owner. Growth begins where blaming ends.

The *owner* asks the only profitable question: "What's in me? Why did I choose to do that or feel that way?" *Notice please* that an owner does not excuse or explain away obvious misconduct on the part of others. Owners may well think of the behavior of others as regrettable or even destructive. But owners know that they can only change themselves. They may be inclined to help the offending party, but they are even more interested in their own personal response. When owners are cut off in traffic, they ask something like this: "When that other driver cut in front of me, why did I honk my horn repeatedly? Why did I get so upset and decide to give him a disgusted look at the next stoplight? What perception, attitude, or habit prompted that response? Did I see that other driver as rude and dangerous? Did it ever occur to me that he might be rushing off to a sick child in the hospital? Or even if he really is just out for himself, why don't I feel sorry for him?" If we do ask such questions, we will certainly get to know much more about ourselves.

Of course, I am not always the owner I would like to be. Like many others, I also resort to blaming, to shifting the responsibility for my own responses. But let me insert here a true story about a time when I did "own" and did learn about myself.

After class one day, two of my students almost playfully remarked to me, "Do you know that you come across to some people as a phony?" I felt anger arising in me, but I know better than to "blow my cool." I'm too controlled for that. So with the precision of a surgeon probing with a scalpel, I asked, "Oh, really, and what does *phony* mean?" They protested that *they* did not think this. They tried to apologize, but I was relentless. "Oh, I heard what you said, but I was just wondering about the meaning of the word *phony.*" Eventually I coaxed out of them the response I was waiting for: "I guess it means that you do not practice what you preach."

Affecting a humble posture, I immediately pleaded guilty. "Oh, in that case, I am a phony. My ideals are just too high for me." I even quoted Saint Paul about "another law warring in my members." (I laugh when I think of myself doing all this.) Then I had to put the final bruise on them. Shylock was looking for his pound of flesh. "There is another meaning of *phony,* my friends. It is that I don't mean what I preach. To this I plead innocent. I do believe what I preach. I just can't practice it as well as I would like." After everybody was quite uncomfortable, we left one another.

The blamer that I too often am would have recalled how he gives his very life to his students. He would have wondered how anyone could be so ungrateful for his gift. He would probably have raved to others about his experience with those two "hopeless adolescents." He would have generated a lot of gastric juice, and held a grudge of resentment that would keep his blood pressure elevated. He would have dug a deeper and deeper rut for himself. I think I was tempted to do this.

Fortunately for me, on this occasion I did not for long remain a blamer. I soon became an owner. I went to my room and sat there alone with my thoughts. "Why did I get angry?" I peeled back the cover of my anger to look inside at the perception under it. After twenty minutes of self-examination, it all became clear. I got angry because I am a phony in the second sense. I recalled many times when I said things and later wondered if I really meant them. I recalled giving a great sermon about death on one occasion. "What do we have to fear? O death, where is your victory? O death, where is your sting?" In the middle of my Oscar-winning performance, I got a sudden stab of pain in the center of my chest. My stomach started tightening. Fear ran up and down my spinal cord. My panic was screaming from a place deep inside me: "This could be a heart attack." But my mouth went right on with the serene sermon.

Of course, the pain quickly passed. But later, when no one could see me, I smiled and mused to myself: "Gee, my stomach and my mouth are only sixteen inches apart, and they are not connected." I laughed to myself: "It's really hard to live with yourself after a good sermon."

Many other such recollections tumbled out of my memory. But the lasting profit was this: I knew why I was angry. My students had stumbled across an exposed nerve. I am a fraction. Part of me believes what I say. Part of me has doubts. Later, in spite of their protestations that it wasn't necessary, I apologized and explained to the two young people. I told them why I had been angry and what I had learned about myself. They said, and I agreed, "That's good, isn't it?"

Blaming Is Like Active Alcoholism

In the last ten years of my life, I think I have learned more from the Alcoholics Anonymous Fellowship than from any other human source. I am not myself an alcoholic, so I feel like a lucky kid who won a free pass to the movies. I get to see the show without having to pay the admission price. One of the things I have learned is that chemically dependent people do not mature while they are drinking or drugging. It is a fact that "being in contact with reality" is an indispensable condition for growing up. When alcohol or drugs separate people from reality, those persons can no longer "tell it like it is" or "see it like it is." They are arrested in their human development. One of my college students, who had been drinking heavily for five or six years prior to his recent sobriety, continually reminded me, "You've got to remember: I didn't have an adolescence." This young man had to pick up the pieces and start to grow again after five or six years of being in an alcoholic haze.

The same thing happens to a blamer. Refusing to take responsibility for one's life and responses is a barrier between that person and reality. It is the barrier of projection and rationalization. It is a haze of ego-defense. Self-deception becomes an escape route. The blamer, like the active alcoholic, does not grow up. Active alcoholics construct their own foggy world. They are at peace only when they are "stoned." In the case of blamers, it is a world of false explanations for true facts. They search for peace by shifting the responsibility for their life and happiness to others.

Does This Apply to Everyone?

What we have been saying about full responsibility applies to all human beings, but in graduated form. When we are infants and small children, we are like soft wax, ready to take on any imprint. Our memory tapes came blank, and in this period they are being filled in. Our perceptions and emotional reactions were for the most part learned from adult influences. At least we learned from our interpretations of those influences.

At the same time we know that children must gradually be given freedom to think and choose for themselves. In a similar way, we must learn in graduated steps to assume full responsibility for our lives and for our happiness. It is an important part of the human process, of our human developmental tasks. We know what would happen if parents insisted on making all the decisions for their children until those children were twenty-one years of age. The result would be some seriously immature twenty-one-year-olds. We also know what would happen if children were taught by example to assign the responsibility for their lives to others. They would remain children all their lives.

So, full responsibility is adult responsibility. But it has to be taught early in life and assumed more and more as we get older. The penalty for refusal is to remain imprisoned in a perpetual childhood.

I am trying to practice what I preach. Sometimes I am successful. At other times I still fail. However, I am making an effort to assume full responsibility for my life and my happiness. I referred earlier to a sign in my mirror which I see and read every morning:

YOU ARE LOOKING AT THE FACE OF THE PERSON
WHO IS RESPONSIBLE FOR YOUR HAPPINESS!

All of life is a process. We are all on a journey to the fullness of life. And we are meant to enjoy the trip. I am sure that the two legs on which we need to walk through life are the first two practices outlined here: (1) joyful self-acceptance—an appreciation of our human uniqueness, and (2) a willingness to assume full responsibility for every step and misstep along the way.

Processing These Ideas about Full Responsibility

1. *Write a Letter of Apology.* Write to all your favorite "blamees" (one letter to cover all). This letter would include not only other persons but also groups, situations, and even inanimate things. Tell them that you are sorry for making them your scapegoats. In your letter admit that it was a big mistake to shift onto them responsibility for your responses. Reassure them that from now on you are going to be an owner. Please remember that this does *not* mean that others were faultless or flawless. It does *not* imply that certain situations were not difficult. It means only that even in dealing with flawed persons and difficult situations, we are still responsible for our own responses. It acknowledges only that something in us determines our responses. When our responses have been undesirable, we must find that "something in us" and deal with it. Our *adult* must take charge of our lives.

2. *Make a List.* Include in this listing the difficult persons, situations, and things that are likely to come back into your life. Using the technique called positive imagining, try to visualize in your imagination as vividly as possible the usual scenario. In this "practice session" try to respond as the person you would like to become. See and hear yourself responding as an owner, not a blamer. Your *adult,* not your *parent* or *child,* is in charge of all your responses. If the practice is successfully repeated a few times, the actual response when the situation is real will be "just like practice." You will become in fact the fully responsible person you have practiced being on the stage of your imagination.

3. *Recall and Record.* Who are some good role models of full self-responsibility in your life? Recall some people you know who are especially good at assuming self-responsibility. How does each of these people demonstrate this acceptance of responsibility in relationships? Ask yourself to put this in writing.

Remember

Growth begins where blaming ends.

We must try to fulfill our needs for relaxation, exercise, and nourishment.

We human beings are not grounded angels or pure spirits trapped in a prison of flesh. Neither are we merely material beings—$1.50 worth of highly organized chemicals. It's just not that simple. The fact is that we are a magnificent oneness that has three interconnected parts: body, mind, *and* spirit. Now this can all get very confusing at times. We want to divide and conquer. We want to uncomplicate this oversized, human mystery. We don't like this interrelationship of parts. We are reluctant to admit that the material body could influence how we think and what we choose. We are likewise reluctant to admit that mind and spirit can work out their hidden agendas on the poor body. We want to deny this kind of oneness and interconnectedness.

Still, it is true: The twisted mind and the deprived spirit can make us physically sick. We laugh at the thought that a simple headache might be the result of a "denied" worry or a crippling attitude of the mind. But, like it or not, it is a fact: We are a mysterious

*oneness with three sensitively interconnected parts.
The body has an effect on mind and spirit. Mind affects body and spirit. And spirit affects body and mind.
And so caring for these bodies of ours is indirectly
caring for mind and spirit. Such caring will always
be necessary for a full and happy life.*

The History of the Separation

In this matter we come by our prejudices quite naturally. The
denial of the interconnectedness of our parts goes all the way
back to the ancient Greek philosophers. Plato was the first to
divide human nature into separate categories. He obviously
thought of the mind (the thinking self) as the superior part of the
human composite. He conceived the mind as separate and distinct
from the body. And he concluded that the body could not influence the mind and vice versa. Then Augustine, Western civiliza-
tion, and Christian thinkers all added their contributions to this
impression that mind and body are separate and distinct. Finally,
it was the philosopher René Descartes who drew a dark black line
of separation between soul and body. Descartes wanted to make
human nature as clear as his beloved geometry. This "Cartesian
dualism" (soul/body) has lasted right up to the present day. Body
is body and soul is soul. It's not mind-body-spirit = one me.

Our past may have been misleading. In us spirit and matter
are not like oil and water. Like it or not, we are a mysterious
oneness. Our bodies and minds and spirits are the sensitively
interconnected parts of this oneness. Nothing can happen in
one of these parts that does not somehow affect the other two
parts.

For years we have entrusted our bodies to physicians, our
minds to psychiatrists, and our souls to theologians. But now we
can no longer maintain this neat separation. Our physicians sometimes tell us that our aches and pains are not purely physical.
They are psychosomatic. In other words, our pains are in our

bodies but are psychologically induced. On the other hand, our psychiatrists sometimes have to inform us that our depression results from a purely physical condition, like a chemical imbalance or vitamin deficiency. And theologians just may report that our suffering is not really a divine trial but is probably due to a distorted idea of what it means to be human. Our spiritual directors may have to go back to deal with our early psychological programming. Our spiritual problems may have originated in this early programming.

The connection between body, mind, and spirit means that a problem that originates in one part may well show up in another part. A crippling perception may cause a headache. The physical condition of inadequate nutrition may well cause psychological depression. And the unsatisfied hungers of the human spirit may well show up in the sickness of our bodies and our minds.

Our happiness requires that all three of these interconnected parts be cared for. No one can be truly happy unless the needs of all three are provided. In this third practice, of course, we are talking mainly about the body and its needs for *relaxation, exercise,* and *nutrition.* However, because of our interconnectedness, in talking about the needs of the body, we are certainly implying a concern for the mind and the spirit which are also essential parts of each of us.

Stress

We have already said that a physical problem can be the cause of mental and spiritual problems. It is also true that attending to our physical needs facilitates the use of mind and the functions of spirit. One of the main problems that afflicts us today is stress. It begins with some strain, tension, or temporary loss of inner harmony. It throws off our sense of balance, or equilibrium. This stress is clearly a fact of life. No one can avoid it. The events or situations that cause stress can be positive and seemingly pleasant as well as negative. Any new challenge will require some adaptation, and this alone can produce stress. Although we humans

usually thrive on growth, we also crave balance and the security
of our equilibrium, the serenity of a steady and unchallenged state.
And so a new child in a family can cause as much stress as a death
in the family. "Falling in love" can be as stressful as "falling out of
love." However, whether its source be pleasant or painful, stress
can easily make us very unhappy.

The four basic sources through which stress enters our lives
are—

- our environment,
- our bodies,
- our minds, and
- our spirits.

As far as *environment* is concerned, there is always some
challenge of adaptation. We are called upon to endure cold and
heat, noise, crowding, living with one another, time deadlines,
threats to personal security and self-esteem. Our *bodies,* too, offer
us many challenges that result in stress: the rapid development
of adolescence, the slow toll of aging, illness, accidents, sleep or
diet disturbances. The *mind* and its various perceptions also can
give rise to stress. For example, we perceive ourselves as inadequate or unloved. We think of ourselves as underdogs or unwor-
thy. We conceive our failures as catastrophic. We interpret reality
as threatening. In each case the result is stress!

And finally, a deprived *spirit* can cause us great discomfort.
We think we can get along without the security and comfort of
faith and its overview. But without these we soon experience a
painful loneliness and anxiety. We fall into a puzzling state of
depression. Something in us wants to know where we have come
from, what we are doing here, and where we are going. The spirit
registers stress when we can't find meaning in life. We don't want
to think of ourselves as mere mortals walking through the motions
of meaningless lives. Just as the body can be sick and cause stress,
so the spirit can become starved and lead us into a stress-filled
vacuum.

As soon as stress occurs in us, whatever its source, there are
immediate biochemical changes that take place in our bodies.

We experience the "fight or flight" response. Our minds perceive some kind of distress or threat. Our regulating physical centers send immediate information throughout the body. The chemicals that carry this message tell the body to speed up its organic and glandular processes to prepare us to deal with or to escape the threat. Only in the last twenty years has medical science discovered the existence of the chemical messengers known as neurotransmitters. The effect is that the pupils of the eyes dilate so we can see better. The hearing becomes more acute. Muscles tense up in order to deal with this perceived new threat. The heart and respiratory rates increase. Blood leaves the extremities and starts pooling in the torso and head. Consequently, the hands and feet grow cold and sweaty.

If the stress is prolonged, these physical conditions become chronic. Psychologically, under stress everything looms out of proportion. Things that ordinarily don't bother us become torturous. We have a hard time concentrating. Sleeping and eating are also affected by chronic stress. We can adapt either by sleeping and eating excessively or by sleeping and eating only fitfully.

Eventually, chronic or repeated stress wears down the body. It is a proven fact that stress always tends to shut down the immune system. So we get sick and we sometimes die. For example, chronic stress can also result in elevated or high blood pressure or hypertension. About 25 million Americans are thought to have hypertension, although half of this number don't even know of the condition. Stress is frequently found as the major cause for respiratory infections, arthritis, colitis, diarrhea, asthma, uneven heart rhythms, many sexual problems, circulatory problems, and even cancer. The doctors of the American Academy of Psychosomatic Medicine, which was founded in 1953, believe that 75 to 90 percent of all reported diseases are due in part to stress. The three best-selling prescription drugs in America are Valium for relaxation, Inderal for high blood pressure, and Tagamet for ulcers. Leaders in industry estimate that 50 to 75 billion dollars are lost each year due to stress-related symptoms. It would seem that many of us are like an accident or an explosion looking for a place to happen.

"Mens Sana in Corpore Sano"

The ancient Latin adage and prescription for happiness was "a healthy mind in a healthy body." Modern science, which has explained stress so clearly to us, has also insisted that we can conquer stress. The vicious circle can be broken. However, to do this, we must learn to relax, to exercise, and to eat a properly balanced diet. The ancients were right: a healthy body contributes greatly to a happy mind and a healthy spirit. These, we remember, are our sensitively interconnected parts.

To be convinced of the importance of the physical, try to recall how you reacted to a given stimulus when you were relaxed. Then recall how you have reacted to the same stimulus when tense, tired, or hungry. Oftentimes it isn't the big things that cause us tension and stress. It's the snapped shoelace when you don't have time to find another. When driving, it is the turn you "can't miss." Stress and the tension it produces magnify all these small irritations of life. We usually don't trip over mountains but molehills. Stress and tension lure us into the telescope trap. Everything begins to look and feel oversized.

The body reacts immediately to any stress, whatever its source. Overwork, the loss of a job, a death or a divorce can easily cause chronic stress. But small things like a time deadline, a simple quarrel, or a gadget that doesn't work can throw us off balance. The message of "Stress!" is immediately carried along neuron, or nerve, tracks and stimulates an increased production of the chemicals of tension. The effects are almost immediate. When the body becomes tense, the functions of mind and spirit are immediately diminished.

Relaxation

The first step in combating stress is to relax. And the first step in learning how to relax is to recognize our stressors. At your first opportunity make a list of the people, the activities, and the situations that tend to create stress in you. Also, most of us have what is known as a "target organ" of stress. It will help you to detect stress more easily if you can identify your target organ and attend to its signals. Some of us get headaches; others get backaches. Some are troubled by stomach upsets; others get skin rashes. With me, it is my sinuses. When I begin to feel pressure in my sinuses, I know it is time to shift into a slower gear. My very personal problem is detecting stress as it builds in me. I am such a determined and driven person. A real "Type A." Stress often gathers hurricane force in me before I am able to recognize it. (I hope you are better at this than I.)

Some stressors seem to help us; others tend to diminish us. Stress in our lives has been compared to the friction of a violin bow. If there is no friction, there is also no music. If there is too much friction, there is only a painful screeching. Helpful stress gets us going. Helpful stress situations seem to excite us and energize us. I have often thought that going into a classroom to teach is a helpful stressor for me. I almost always feel stimulated by the prospect.

Relaxing by Converting Stressors

Some stressors that tend to be destructive can be converted into helpful stressors. For example, most of us find only a destructive stress in harboring resentment. We tend to judge harshly those whom we resent. We try to avoid them, if possible. If we have to deal with them, we try to conceal our resentment, but afterward we feel drained. It has been wisely said that if you want to be a slave to someone, resent that person. He or she will be with you in the morning, throughout the day, and into the night. The resented person will eat with you and ruin your digestion. He or she will destroy your powers of concentration, ruin your good times, and deprive you of your precious peace and joy.

How do I go about converting the stress of resentment? Can it be changed into a helpful stress? Something that helps me very much is the realization that in resenting another, I have put my happiness into the hands of that person. I have given that person a very real power over me. The change from a negative to a positive charge will take place at the moment I truly take back the responsibility for my own happiness. This usually means that I must forgive the person I resent. I have to release that person from the real or imagined debt owed me, and I have to release myself from the high price of continued resentment.

I think that true and complete forgiveness depends on this insight: "Everyone makes psychological sense." There is always so much I do not know and will never know about those I tend to resent. To understand these people, I would have to know about their genes, family, education, experiences, neighborhood, and so forth. As noted earlier, the human brain weighs three pounds, three ounces. But it stores within itself more messages than the most sophisticated computer ever built. Whenever a human being acts, all the messages that have been stored in the brain are somehow activated. They all feed into every action and reaction. So I can never be sure how much any person really needs forgiveness. Maybe if I could know all the messages fed into and stored in that person's brain, I would be sympathetic rather than critical. The bottom line: I just don't know.

I must always plead ignorance. Then to the extent that the person needs my forgiveness, I give it. God knows, I am myself often in need of the same understanding forgiveness that I need to offer. In the end of the forgiveness process, I will feel sorry for, not angry at, the offending person. I will be at peace because I will have released both of us from the bondage of resentment. I will have reclaimed responsibility for my own happiness. To the extent that I am able to accomplish this, my negative stress will be converted into a positive and helpful stress.

To take another example, some teachers get bent out of shape when a student disagrees with them. I have often fallen into this trap myself. There is another insight here: "In a win-lose argument, everyone loses." However, asking the student to elaborate on his or her point of view can lead to a meaningful sharing. In sharing, everyone wins. Of course, it calls for abdication from the pretense of looking as if you know everything. That's a hard act to sustain anyway. If, in spite of all this, the student is still unpleasant or arrogant, it pays to remember that "an obnoxious person is a hurting person." Such insights can well be the "converters" we need in dealing with stress.

The same kind of conversion process can be applied to the expression of feelings. First we must come to the realization that feelings are not morally good or bad. We must also realize that it is always good for everyone to have fully and to express freely all significant feelings. Otherwise the stomach keeps score, and a bottled-up emotion becomes destructive if not deadly. We are as sick as we are secret. Of course, feelings have to be expressed in "I" not "You" statements. For example, "I felt angry," rather than "You made me angry!" Obvious insights and simple skills can produce the miracle of conversion quite easily. Harmful stress becomes helpful stress. Tranquillity replaces tension.

So, first we must learn to identify our stressors. The transformation of a negative stressor into a positive stressor is something like the experience of a miracle. What was hurtful becomes helpful. We can often gain the enlightenment and empowerment to make this conversion by talking the matter over with another. It is especially helpful if that person has experienced the same stress and has successfully gone through the conversion process.

Relaxing by Techniques

Obviously, not all negative stressors can be converted into positive stressors. For example, the death of a dear one means that we must go through a grieving process. There is no shortcut through this sorrow. There is no way to make grief pleasant. And so it is helpful to find ways to release such tensions. Whether our tensions result from major grief or from everyday stress, we all need to practice and use some helpful form of relaxation. There are many of these, and each person has to use whatever seems to help.

One common technique is to set aside some time each day for a hobby that has a pacifying, relaxing effect. At the end of each day I usually play the piano and relax. I am a musician in the same sense that a woodpecker is a carpenter. My music would definitely not relax someone who knows and loves music, but it does relax me. Other hobbies that might appeal to you are baking, gardening, reading, talking, listening to music, collecting, looking through photo albums, writing, and so forth.

Still another popular technique is to make a daily appointment with yourself. During this appointment time, try to learn to enjoy the peace of doing nothing. See if it helps. Sit back and close your eyes. Breathe deeply, all the way in and all the way out. Imagine yourself in a place of peace, a delightful place you have actually visited or can easily imagine. Feel all your muscles unstretching. Relax and enjoy this daily appointment with yourself. It's cheaper and better than Valium.

Some final suggestions on relaxation:

1. Find a confidant with whom you can be totally open and feel totally safe. Please don't cop out and say that you just cannot find one. With a little coaching, almost any well-intentioned person will do. Talk out all your significant and emotion-filled experiences. But be sure you let your confidant have equal time. Nobody wants to be a human garbage dump for emotional refuse.
2. Take a walk through the world of nature. Take time to examine and smell the flowers. Watch and listen to the waves of water at the lake or ocean. Look up at and admire the stars.
3. Reread a favorite book or poem.
4. Describe in a journal the most recent storm or crisis in your life, and be sure to add what you have learned from the experience. There is always a positive side to every storm or crisis.
5. Write in a journal daily. Let the subject matter concern your thoughts, feelings, and needs.
6. Remember your favorite jokes and laugh. Humor is healing.

Physical Exercise

The traditional formula for tension is, "An overactive mind in an underactive body." Daily, vigorous (if possible) exercise restores the balance. It also releases the buildup of tension. What exercise does for us physically is clear out of the brain and bloodstream the chemicals of tension. Exercise also promotes the production and flow of the chemicals that make us feel relaxed and peaceful, like the endorphines. It is very difficult to be depressed after vigorous exercise. Joggers often experience a feeling of exhilaration, commonly called runners' high. Physically, it is a neuro-chemical change in the body brought about by exercise.

It is interesting to note what many authors on the mid-life crisis recommend above and before all: daily, vigorous exercise. Often psychological or spiritual needs assert themselves most forcibly at mid-life. The result is not only the intrusion of our old friend, stress, but a vicious circle that apparently traps many of us. We get into the circle when our needs produce stress, and then the stress magnifies the needs. The result is more stress. The quickest way out is daily, vigorous exercise. Jog, swim, walk briskly, but do something!

More than fifteen years ago, I took the heart examination called a stress test. It was a blessing in disguise. I got onto the treadmill, while my heart was being monitored by an attending physician. I was convinced that the test would be a mere routine and that everything would go well. However, after six or seven minutes, the doctor stopped the machine. He asked me to sit down with my feet up. He kept listening attentively with his stethoscope to the sounds of my heart. Finally, he said that everything was back to normal. He explained that my heart had started to "palpitate." It was working very hard without achieving very much. He suggested that it might well be due to "lack of exercise."

And that was the beginning of my career as a jogger. I started out by running very slowly for a short distance. (Old men walking their dogs often passed me.) Then I would walk until I could comfortably resume running. Eventually my capacity increased, and I now jog for three or four miles every day. (I still have to be careful of those old men and their dogs.) The day I took up jogging was indeed "the first day of the rest of my life." The "running doctor," cardiologist Dr. George Sheehan, has said that jogging may not increase the length of your life, but it will certainly improve the quality of your life. Beyond all doubt, jogging has done this for me.

The human body is a strange machine. It wears out from *lack of use*. Strangely enough, human energy comes into existence through the use of our bodies or exercise. Consequently, physical fitness contributes greatly to the energy we have to expend. Very often the best remedy for tiredness or weariness is a half hour of aerobic exercise. Inaction tends to make us sluggish. It actually leads to low energy, depression, and despair. It's hard to believe, but we can't hoard energy; that is, we can't build up our supply of energy by not using it. Of course, adequate rest is essential, but if it is not accompanied by physical activity, rest can prove depressing for most of us. Unused energy, like untapped potential, turns into a destructive force. I think it is safe to say that everyone can profit from physical exercise. We can all increase our energy supply by exercise.

Ever since researchers began examining the effects of physical exercise, its benefits have been firmly established. The death rate from cancer and heart disease has always been highest among people whose work involves the least amount of physical exertion. On the other end of the spectrum, the death rate from cancer and heart problems has been lowest among those whose work involves the greatest amount of physical exertion. (Cf. *The Healing Family* by Stephanie Matthews Simonton and Robert L. Shook [Bantam Books, 1984]).

Of course, not everyone can or wants to jog. But almost everyone can walk briskly. Brisk walking has virtually all the benefits of strenuous exercise. Like jogging or swimming, brisk walking raises the metabolism so that the body burns up calories at a faster rate. It improves muscle tone and the efficiency of the heart. Exercise has also been found to lessen the buildup of plaque in the arteries, to lower blood pressure, and to slow down the aging process. With all these obvious benefits, exercise has to be a considerable factor in human happiness.

Stress and tension are greatly reduced by regular physical exercise. Consequently, those who exercise see a peaceful and proportioned world. They tend to have a healthy perspective.

They think more clearly, remember better, and are more cheerful, pleasant, and optimistic. Of course, getting started may be the most difficult part. But the eventual rewards are enormous.

Nourishment: The Engine Won't Work Unless Properly Fueled

If we are to be happy and fully alive, good nutrition is absolutely essential. Keeping fit through right eating is very important. The human engine just won't run smoothly unless it is properly fueled. I know that it sounds overdramatic to link our social ills to nutrition. However, from crime and insanity to divorce and drug addiction, there is a connection. The late Adelle Davis, one of the most respected nutritionists of our times, wrote:

> We can expect all of these social problems to increase, involving ever larger percents of our population, unless our nutrition is markedly improved. I am not saying for a minute that faulty nutrition is the *only* cause of these social ills . . . but inadequate nutrition is still a vital factor which has received, as Dr. Margaret Mead puts it, "nearly total inattention." (*Let's Eat Right to Keep Fit* [Harcourt Brace Jovanovich, 1970], p. 248)

The body is obviously the instrument through which the mind and spirit work. One dramatic instance and proof of this is brain damage. The powers to know and choose are powers of the mind and spirit. But if the brain is damaged, as in the case of accident victims or punch-drunk boxers, the powers of the mind and spirit can be very limited. Likewise, it is true that if the brain is nutritionally deprived, the same effects will follow in proportion. In the case of prolonged alcoholism, the brain eventually turns to "mush." Another example: vitamin B_6 is necessary for the normal functioning of the brain. When this vitamin is withheld from diets in an attempt to starve cancer cells, convulsions result both in children and in adults.

An Eastern Parable

There is an Eastern parable of a horse, carriage, and driver that is a good illustration of the human condition and human interconnectedness. The carriage in this parable is the human body. The horse represents the human emotions, and the driver is the mind.

If the system does not function well, the first thing to check out is the care and condition of the carriage. If it has not been oiled and exercised, it may be that parts of the carriage are rusty or rotting. Maintenance may be poor, and lack of proper care and usage may have created further deterioration. This carriage has a built-in system of self-lubrication. The bumps of the road are supposed to help circulate these lubricants. However, if the carriage has not been cared for or exercised, it may be that many of its joints have become frozen or corroded. Its appearance may even be shabby and unattractive. Obviously, for safe and efficient travel the carriage must be well maintained.

Consequently, many psychotherapists recommend a program of relaxation, nourishment, and exercise as a starting point. If the ride through life is proving uncomfortable, the first place to check out is the maintenance of the carriage (body). It may well be that the problem is here. If problems persist, a good psychotherapist will then proceed to check out the horse (emotions) and the driver (mind). However, "seemingly deeper" problems often disappear after the body has been properly relaxed, nourished, and exercised.

Conclusion

There is much in our historically rooted prejudices that wants to deny the interaction of body, mind, and spirit. And yet this sensitive interconnectedness is daily dramatized in our own experience. When we are overstressed, we become irritable. When we are physically underexercised, we get "down" emotionally. We lose the capacity to think clearly. Under prolonged stress, the very spirit in us is likewise stifled. Attending to our own physical needs for relaxation, exercise, and nourishment makes great sense. Without this care, the quality of our lives is greatly reduced. The world just doesn't make sense, and life begins to feel like a painful treadmill. We begin to ask, "What's it all about, anyway?"

Processing These Ideas about Fulfilling Our Bodily Needs

1. *Make a List.* (Are you ready for another list?) This time you are asked to list the things you have done in the last week to care for your body. Use the categories of *relaxation, exercise,* and *nutrition.* Then give yourself a mark for your body-caring efforts. A = awe-inspiring, B = beautiful, C = coming along, D = dragging along, and F = fooling yourself.

2. *Choose an Accountability Partner.* A close friend will no doubt be happy to join you in this process. Determine that you and this partner will check in with each other at regular intervals. Make out a set of three resolutions, one concerning each of the following: *relaxation, exercise,* and *nutrition.* Share these with your accountability partner, and promise to talk regularly about your successes or failures. Make signs to remind yourself of these resolutions. Put these signs in your mirror, on bookmarks, on your personal bulletin board. Sure, it will ask a gritty perseverance of you. But please remember: The only programs that work are the programs we are willing to work at.

3. *Locate Your Stressors.* On the list below, check off the signs of stress that you regularly experience. Some of the following are physical and others are emotional. All are signals, saying something to you about relaxation, exercise, or nutrition.

- muscular tension
- headaches
- skin problems
- chest pains
- cold extremities (hands and feet)
- abnormal eating habits

- trembling
- dizziness
- pounding heart
- troubled breathing
- psychosomatic illnesses (hypertension, ulcers, hives, frequent colds)
- frequent tiredness in spite of sufficient sleep
- inability to sleep well
- nervousness
- frequent anger, irritability
- frequent "frazzled" or "drained" feeling
- burnout: "I just can't take it anymore."
- inability to slow down
- inability to enjoy, to laugh
- constant "keyed-up" feeling
- frequent anxiety, fear, worry
- inability to concentrate
- restlessness
- difficulty in getting along with others
- frequent daydreaming
- the frequent desire to avoid recurring situations
- no appetite, excessive appetite

After setting out on a program of relaxation, exercise, and nourishment, look again at the symptoms you have just checked. Notice that they have diminished or disappeared.

Remember

It's hard to be happy when you're traveling through life in a tense or tired chassis. So begin. Everything else is easy.

We must make our lives an act of love.

For those who have not loved, old age is a wintertime of loneliness. The greatest human talent was buried in the ground so it would not be lost. And in the end everything was lost. No one else came or cared. There was only a loveless person and a lonely waiting for death.

+For those who have loved, old age is a harvest time. The seeds of love planted so carefully and so long ago have matured with time. The loving person is surrounded in the twilight of life with the presence and the caring of others. The bread always comes back on the waters. What was given so freely and joyfully has been returned with interest.

What Is Love?

If there is a more frequently misused word in our English language, I don't know what it is. Most young people and many of us who are old enough to know better think of love as a *feeling*. When a feeling turns us on, we speak of "falling in love." When the feeling ebbs, love is suddenly but clearly a matter of history. It's over. An infatuation, or temporary emotional attraction, can so easily be confused with love.

Another source of confusion is that almost all of us at some time misconstrue *need* for *love*. When another person comes along and fills one of our needs, we are tempted to say, "Oh, I love you." The classic expression of real love, "I need you because I love you," is very much different from "I love you because I need you." You do not earn my love by filling my emptiness, my need. My love is always my freely given gift to you.

Real love, I feel sure, is a *decision* and a *commitment*. Before I can really love someone, I must make an inner decision which commits me to whatever is best for the one I love. Love moves me to say, to do, to be whatever the one loved needs. Love may ask me to be tough or tender, to be blue velvet or blue steel. Love may ask me to confront the one I love, or it may ask me to console that person. But I must first say yes to love. I must make that decision and commitment. Whatever love asks of me, I must be ready to do. At the crossroads of every decision, I must ask only this: "What is the loving thing to do?"

Is this possible? Of course, it is not possible to be perfect at anything. But it is an excellent ideal. In fact, it is the only life principle that can bring us happiness. At every moment in my life and yours, we are asking a fundamental question. This question concerns our life principle. I may be asking, "How can I make the most money?" Or it may be that I am asking, "Where will I have the most fun?" The person who has decided to make his or her life an act of love does not ask primarily about money or fun. The loving person does not ask about pleasure, does not listen for applause or sniff for incense. The basic drive of this person is simply to be a loving human being. The only question is, "What is the loving thing to do?" This is the decision of love. This is love's commitment.

Love at Different Levels

Of course, love can exist at many levels. Some people in my life take precedence over others. The "commitment" level is deeper in some cases, as in a marriage or family. There are strangers, acquaintances, enemies, classmates, coworkers, friends, neighbors, close friends, sisters and brothers, parents, spouses, and children. A loving person tries to read and recognize and fill the needs of all, insofar as he or she is able. However, because there are degrees of closeness, there will also be differing levels of commitment. There is an order of priority, corresponding to the level of commitment. Family before friends. Friends before strangers, and so forth.

Love of Self and Love of Others

Of course, we cannot talk of loving others without first mentioning that love begins at home. We must first love ourselves. The psychiatrist of interpersonal relationships, Harry Stack Sullivan, says that "when the happiness, security, and well-being of another person is as real or more real to you than your own, you love that person." The obvious assumption is that my own happiness, security, and well-being are real to me. In fact, to the extent that I fail to love myself, to that same extent I will be unable to love others.

If I am to be a loving person, I must weigh my own happiness, security, and well-being as well as those of another. I must balance my needs with the needs of others whom I also love. For example, I am hungry and on my way to dinner, or tired and on my way to bed. I meet you, and you express a need to talk. I have to ask you how important, how urgent it is for you to talk at this time. If it is a minor matter, I may make an appointment to see you tomorrow. My needs will take priority over yours. However, if you have just suffered a serious setback, a death in the family, or if you are suicidal, my dinner or sleep can wait. Your needs will take priority over mine. A loving person will be called on to make many difficult decisions, and this prioritizing is surely one of them.

Most of the other love decisions have to do with the "good of the one loved." What is really good for you may not be what you would prefer. You may be getting drunk, for example, and ask me to get you another drink. Or you may ask me to join you in a lie or deception. Likewise, you may be a shy person and ask me to ignore you. I must say no to all of these requests. Another example would be the case of the emotional bully. You may want to "walk all over" me or to tell me off abusively. You may try to manipulate me with your anger or your tears. Love will ask me in these cases not to give one inch. Love forbids me to be a "door-mat" or a "dingbat." Love may ask me to confront you or to walk away from you. So whatever else we might say of love, it is definitely not for those who seek the course of least resistance. It is, however, for those who would be happy.

A friend of mine had been a teacher for most of his life. Once he confided to me that he had been an alcoholic for twenty years during his teaching career. During this time, he said, his family and friends made excuses for him. They were classic "enablers," enabling him to go on drinking. Others took his classes when he was too drunk or too hung over to teach. And so his self-destruction by drinking went on for all those years. "Then," he almost sighed with relief, "thank God, someone loved me with a tough love. Someone loved me enough to confront me. He stood right in front of me, and he promised that if I did not get help, he would blow the whistle on me. He said I was sick and that I needed help. He said that he loved me too much to watch me destroy myself. That's what turned me around. So I got help."

My friend's story of being loved with a tough love reminded me of something I once heard: If a loved one comes home in a drunken stupor and falls asleep on the front lawn, the most loving and kind thing to do would be to leave the person there. It is part of his "hitting bottom." The person will change only when he or she is allowed to feel the full impact of pain, to suffer the consequences of drinking. By the way, the cruelest thing would be to turn on the sprinkler.

The Third Object of Love: God

There is a third object of my love, namely, God. Besides myself and others, I must love the Lord my God with my whole mind and heart and strength. Loving God adds a new and different dimension to love. In spite of what we would like to believe, it is a fact that we cannot give God anything that God doesn't already have. God does not need us as we truly need one another. Only those who are needy experience need, and God is not needy. However, God does ask us to love one another. And the Lord promises that whatever we do for the least of his children, he will take as done to himself.

And, of course, God does ask us to accept and to do his will. As I see it, the bottom line in doing God's will seems to be this: Do I make my own plans and then ask God to support those plans? Or do I ask God what are his plans, and then seek to know my place in those plans? To remind myself, I have a second sign in my mirror that thanks God for loving me, and then asks: "What have you got going today? I'd like to be part of it."

Of course, God's will is often mysterious. However, of this we can all be certain: God wants us to use fully all the gifts he has given us. In the second century, Saint Irenaeus wrote that "the glory of God is a person who is fully alive." Have you ever given a gift to another and then noticed that the other person never used your gift? Do you remember what you wanted to ask: "Didn't you like the gift I gave you? Why don't you ever use it?" Maybe God wants to ask us about the gifts he has given us. When we say in the Lord's Prayer, "Thy will be done!" I am certain that part of this will is that I stretch to use all my talents. I know that God wills that I should develop my senses, emotions, mind, will, and heart as fully as possible. "The glory of God is a person who is fully alive."

Something in me is sure that our love for God is measured totally by our willingness to do these two things: to love one another as we love ourselves, and to do God's will in all things.

The Three Parts
of Loving One Another

It has been rightly said that there are three parts of the love we are asked to give one another. They are (1) *kindness,* (2) *encouragement,* and (3) *challenge.* Only the mind and heart of love know when each is needed by the one loved. But these three parts of love seem in general to build on one another in the order given. If I am to love you effectively, I must first of all make it clear to you that I care, that I am on your side. I am committed to be "for you." This is the message of *kindness.* Once this is established, I must go on to encourage you to believe in yourself. Letting you lean on me or hitchhike on my strength is not loving you. It is keeping you weak and dependent. I must help you to use your own strength by urging you to think and choose for yourself. This is the task of *encouragement.* And finally, after kindness and encouragement have been successfully offered, I must challenge you to put your goodness and giftedness to work. You know I care. You know I believe in you and that I am sure you can do it. Now I say, "Do it. Go ahead, do it!" It is the moment of *challenge.*

And so Erich Fromm has appropriately called *loving* an *art.* In sciences, as in recipes, there are exact measures and careful directions for procedure. Not so in love. I must artfully decide when it is time for kindness, when encouragement is needed, and when the person I love is ready for challenge. There are no manuals of instruction, no certain answers, only my best judgment. At times I may misfire in my judgment. But I can always apologize for my failures. And others can always accept my good intentions, even when my judgment has been poor.

True Love Is Unconditional

One of the requisites that true love must fulfill is that it be *unconditional*. The opposite, conditional love, is not really love. It is a barter. "I will love you as long as . . . until . . . if you . . ." The contract is filled with fine print, and the one to whom this conditional "love" is offered is asked to conform to all the provisions. Otherwise, the contract is null and void. Conditional love is threatening. It may be taken away for one misstep. Conditional love is "pan-scale" love. "If you put your donation on one of the pans, I will put my contribution on the other. But I won't be cheated. I'm watching you. If you don't go 50 percent of the way, neither will I." Of course, such "love" is a counterfeit. It never survives.

I think that a lot of the anger we see in the world is the result of this conditional love. In the end, we tend to resent someone who has "loved" us in this conditional way. We feel used. We want to protest, "You never really loved me. You loved my pretty face as long as it was pretty. You loved my clean clothes and demanded that I keep them clean. You loved my good marks and made it clear that I was not allowed to fail. You loved my abilities. But you never loved *me*. I was always walking on egg shells. I knew that if I ever failed to meet your requirements, you would treat me as a smoker treats cigarettes. You would use me up, grind me out, and throw me away."

Love and Unfaithfulness

So love is by its nature unconditional. But what if I set out to love someone and that person is repeatedly unfaithful to me? Does unconditional love just forgive again and again and continue to love? This is a good question and should be addressed, but the answer is not easy. Love certainly does not ask me to become stupid or naive. So I have to make the judgment—as best I can— about what would be the loving thing to do, to be, to say. Forgiveness is not the real issue here. Of course, I forgive you. Love sets no limits to forgiveness. The real issue is, "What is best for you and for me?" That is what I must do.

I must try to balance my love for myself and my love for you. I must ask, "What is the best way to preserve my own self-esteem and out of love to help you at the same time?" Love is indeed an art and not a science. There are no clear and obvious answers. Love does not promise us a rose garden.

Certainly, to write you off because you have disappointed me would be a thinly veiled form of conditional love. On the other hand, to go on trusting you after repeated unfaithfulness would not be loving you. It would only enable you to stay weak. It would also not be loving myself. It would certainly tend to undermine my own self-respect. So I have to ask myself this hard question: Considering all the circumstances, what would be the best thing to say, to do, to be, for you *and* for me? At a certain point, I think, I would have to ask you to choose between faithfulness with me or unfaithfulness without me.

Love Includes . . .
Love Excludes

Sometimes it is agonizing to answer the questions love asks. It may be helpful first to consider this question: What does love include and what does love exclude? Saint Paul, in his First Letter to the Corinthians, gives us a few suggestions:

> The love of which I speak is slow to lose patience.
> It always looks for a way to be constructive.
> Love is not possessive.
> Neither is it anxious to impress,
>   nor does it cherish inflated ideas
>   of its own importance.
> Love has good manners
>   and does not pursue selfish advantage.
> Love is not touchy or fragile.
> It does not keep an account of evil,

or gloat over the wickedness of other people.
On the other hand, love is glad
    with all good people whenever truth prevails.
Love does not give up on others.
Love knows no end to its trust, no fading of its hope.
Love outlasts everything.
Love is in fact the one thing
    that will still be standing when all else has fallen.

Paraphrase of 1 Corinthians 13:4-8

My own list goes something like this:

What LOVE DOES	**What LOVE DOESN'T**
LOVE ACCEPTS you wherever you are	LOVE DOESN'T ABUSE you or take you for granted
AFFIRMS your goodness and giftedness	ASK you to march to a different drummer
CARES about you, wants to know that you're okay	BLAME you or carry angry grudges
CHALLENGES you to be all you can be	BULLY you by anger, a loud voice, or tears
EMPATHIZES—knows what it's like to be you	GET you into win-lose arguments
ENCOURAGES you to believe in yourself	GIVE you unsolicited advice
IS GENTLE in its way of dealing with you	JUDGE you or tell you "what your whole trouble is"
KEEPS CONFIDENCES—your secrets are safe	JUST TOLERATE you as a condescending favor
IS KIND—is always for you, on your side	MAKE YOU PROVE yourself again and again
LAUGHS A LOT, always with, never at you	NEED always to be right, to have all the answers
LOOKS FOR GOODNESS in you and finds it	POUT or refuse to talk to you

MAKES YOU FEEL GLAD that you're you

OVERLOOKS your foolish vanities, human weakness

PRAYS for your needs and your growth

SEES good things in you that others had never noticed

SHARES itself with you, by self-disclosure

SPEAKS UP when you need someone to defend you

IS TACTFUL even when confronting you

TAKES RESPONSIBILITY for its own behavior

TELLS YOU THE TRUTH always and honestly

THINKS about you and your needs

IS TOUGH OR TENDER, depending on your needs

UNDERSTANDS your ups and downs, allows you "bad days"

PUNISH you vindictively for being wrong

REMEMBER all the things you have done wrong

SEEK and call attention to itself

SHOW OFF, just to let you know where you stand

UNDERMINE your confidence in yourself

USE you for its own purposes and then discard you

VENTILATE its emotions on you as a garbage dump

WRITE YOU OFF because you didn't meet its demands

(The things that are included here may help to prime your own pump. Please feel free to add, subtract, edit, and borrow. Your own list is the one that will be most meaningful to you.)

Two Gifts for All Seasons

One of the painful questions love asks is, What do you need? The answers will vary from day to day, depending on your life situation and mood. But, it seems to me, two gifts are always in order: *honest self-revelation* and *sincere affirmation*. Being open and totally honest is like offering another a gentle hospitality. "Please come in and make yourself at home with me." Most of us are afraid of what others might think. We are afraid that our openness will be costly. Others might use it later in a hostile way. Of course, we try to rationalize our fears. We build walls of self-protection, on the grounds that "good fences make good neighbors."

One man admitted to his therapist that he hadn't told his wife how he felt because "she has been depressed lately and I didn't want to add to her sadness." A week later, the same man confided to the therapist that he hadn't told his wife how he felt because "she was feeling really good this week and I didn't want to tell her anything that would upset her." The therapist rightfully confronted the poor fellow. "You've got a problem here. I think you are basically afraid to tell her your feelings. You're using any excuse you can in order to cop out."

Love is honest and love is open. But love is also kind and tactful. It would be tragic to pass like ships in the night. But it would also be tragic if we rammed into one another and destroyed one another. Communication really is the secret of successful love relationships. (I have tried to offer some helpful guidelines for successful communication in another book, coauthored with psychotherapist Loretta Brady, *Will the Real Me Please Stand Up?* [Tabor Publishing, 1985].)

The second gift of love that is always in season is *sincere affirmation*. Affirmation is that act by which we help others to appreciate their own goodness and giftedness. We affirm their value as persons, their sense of worth. In the first practice of the ten proposed in this book, we have said that a joyful acceptance of self is absolutely necessary for true happiness. However, no one can sustain this inner joyful acceptance without confirmation from others. I can't believe that I am really a good teacher if my classes consistently tell me otherwise. Most human beings are imprisoned behind walls and masks by the fear of their own inadequacy. No one can believe in his or her unique worth unless there is some recognition of that worth by others. When people are sincerely affirmed, they come to life like a drooping flower that has been watered. I have long believed that the greatest contribution love can make is this sincere affirmation. It is life changing. It can be world changing.

You may remember the story that humorist Art Buchwald wrote about affirmation. It was entitled "My Friend, the Cabbie, and New York City." It seems that Art's friend was determined to change the whole world by starting with New York City. The simple means: *praise* or *affirmation.* So after Art and his friend took a hectic cab ride, the friend complimented the cabbie. "You are one of the best drivers I have ever seen. If you had one more coat of paint on your car, you would have hit several of those other cars. But you missed them, and I want to congratulate you." Of course, the cabbie was startled by this and asked, "What are you? Some kind of nut?" But Buchwald's friend insisted that he was serious. The cabbie drove away, smiling broadly. Later the two men were walking along the street, and Buchwald noticed his friend winking at a passing woman. When Art asked his friend why he did that, the friend replied, "It's part of the program. If she's a schoolteacher, her class is going to have a great day."

Of course, the affirmation we are proposing has to be honest and sincere. People usually see through pretended affirmation. Still, we all find whatever it is we are looking for. And there is so much goodness and giftedness in those around us. This goodness and giftedness may for the most part go unrecognized. It may be desperately crying out for some kind of recognition and affirmation.

The Main Obstacle to Love
Is a Four-Letter Word:
Pain

I remember that a young woman once came to me, contemplating an abortion. She was three months pregnant. I remember describing the condition of her unborn child. I told her how the baby had brain waves, a beating heart. All the physical systems are working at three months. I promised her all the help she would need, if only "you will give your baby a chance at life." I clearly remember how she looked up from the floor, with a searching question on her face. She asked me a question that I very much needed to hear. "I know you love my baby. Do you also love me?" In a flash the insight hit me. She had no love to give her unborn child unless someone loved and cared about her. Her own pains and fears had drained her of her capacity to love another.

Whenever I think of her, I am reminded of a conversation I once had with a psychiatrist friend of mine. I asked him why it was so hard for many of us to love. He smiled at me, with that smile which psychiatrists usually reserve for celibates. He agreed with me that we are made to love, just as we are made to grow up physically. But just as some sicknesses can stunt our physical growth, there is a definite obstacle that prevents us from growing in love. The good doctor asked me, "Did you ever have a toothache?" I admitted that I had. "Who were you thinking about when your tooth was hurting?" he inquired. "Only myself," I replied. "The answer is there," he suggested. "Pain magnetizes all attention to itself, to ourselves. A physical ache, a worry, a failure, grief or remorse—all are painful, and so rob us of our capacity to love. When pain becomes a way of life, the person usually becomes very self-centered."

The hardest time to make one's life an act of love is during a period of pain. The pain seems to attract all our attention, absorb all our energies. There is nothing left over for loving. The well is dry. Most people in pain know only one reality: "I hurt." Only when we have successfully dealt with or endured pain long enough for it to go away are we capable of beginning again to love ourselves and others. It helps to understand this. To name a demon is at least the beginning of successfully dealing with it.

Chronic Unhappiness Represents a Failure to Love

The source of most chronic unhappiness is a failure to love. All the great psychiatrists—Freud, Adler, Jung, Frankl—have said this.

However, this is clearly not meant to imply that the failure is culpable or blameworthy. It may be that my early programming and experiences did not encourage me to love myself, my neighbor, or my God. I may spend much of my life paying the high price of this failure to love. However, it could be that I am only acting out my past programming and experiences. I may be failing to love because of messages that I absorbed from others and from my early life situation.

Of course, we cannot judge human responsibility. But we can say for certain that if a person does not love him or herself, there is only misery ahead. Or it may be that, because of early programming in distrust, a person does not really love others. As long as this condition prevails, there is no real hope for happiness. Such a person lives in a sad and shrunken world that has a population of one. And I must add that the human spirit is seriously deprived without a relationship of love with a loving God. As the French author Leon Bloy once wrote, "Only the saints are truly happy."

Love and the Laboratory of Life

I remember once disliking someone quite intensely. He was the proverbial drop of vinegar in my barrel of sweetness. Long after this person had gone out of my life, the upsetting memory remained. So I was delighted by the visit of a psychologist friend who maintains that if something really bothers you, you have not fully explored the cause of your unhappiness. The cause of your upset is not what you think. If it were, you wouldn't be so upset by it. So I told him about my problem, and we went through his test. First I closed my eyes and relaxed. Then I "unpacked" my brain of everything else, and went through an imaginary door. I took only the problem person and my upsetting memories with me into the room beyond the door. Soon my body was reacting, and according to directions, I dialogued with my physical reactions. What emotion did I push deep down inside myself so that it could get out only as a physical reaction? What I felt in the end was guilt, not anger. When my shoulders sagged and an audible sigh of relief passed from my lips, my psychologist friend knew that I had discovered the real cause of my upset.

What in fact I discovered was that the reason for my inner unrest was that I had never loved but only resented the person in question. I couldn't recall ever feeling sorry for him, or ever asking myself what I could do to help him. I know somewhere deep inside myself that obnoxious people are hurting people. But I did not compassionate his hurting. I spent all my energies resenting the obnoxious symptoms. But I am learning. I know now that resentment is a form of enslavement. I know that the price of making my life an act of love means reversing a lot of my old habits and values. It is difficult, but the alternative is a life of misery—and an old age of loneliness.

Love: God's Gift to Us and Our Gift to God

There are two things I would like to say about love and God. I realize that in our pluralistic society, both of my statements will be vehemently debated. However, I believe that this discussion of a life of love would be incomplete without some inclusion of these two things. These are my beliefs: (1) Love is a gift of God, and (2) When we love, God acts.

Love Really Is a Gift of God

I accept the Bible as the word of God. So I look to the Bible for answers to questions like the one we are now asking. I think that the Bible is quite clear on this point. Love is indeed a gift from God. Saint Paul talks about the three main gifts of God: faith, hope, and love. Then he proclaims that the greatest of these gifts is love. Paul says that there are many and various gifts of God, but the one we should ask for above all else is this gift of love. (See 1 Corinthians, chapters 13 and 14.)

Saint John is even more explicit. He simply says, "Let us love one another, because love comes from God. Whoever loves is a child of God and knows God" (1 John 4:7).

I think I can anticipate your next question: If love is in fact a gift of God, can those who do not believe in God really love? It would take much more time and space than we have to answer that question adequately. But let me say simply: Yes, of course, people without faith are able to love. God believes in many people who do not believe in God. In some cases God gives us gifts, such as the power to love, as a prelude to the gift of faith. At other times God simply enlightens nonbelievers in their love choices and empowers them in their love commitments. A great theologian, Karl Rahner, once referred to such people as "anonymous Christians." And the great Thomas Aquinas insisted that "God is not limited in his gift giving to those who are sacramentally united to him."

To paraphrase Jesus, "God lets the rain fall on the crops of the believers and the nonbelievers. God lets the sun fall on the fields of the believers and also the nonbelievers." If this is true, of what value is faith? For those of us who believe, faith opens us to a loving relationship with God. It enables us to know where our gifts have come from. And, of course, faith wins us further gifts, as we learn from the story of the lady with the hemorrhages. To this woman and to most of the people for whom Jesus worked wonders, he said, "Your faith has made this possible." There is no point in God doing a work of power if it is not going to be recognized. And it is clear to me that it takes faith to recognize a miracle. There were many works of power Jesus could not do because there was no faith in those who surrounded him. God is something like an electrical outlet. There is much power to be had, but only if we are connected. And the connection is faith. Faith releases the power of God.

The importance of knowing that love is a gift from God is this: We will more surely receive this gift when we know that its source is God and not simply a matter of using our own powers. Most of us first have to try our own little formulas for relationships of love. Eventually we come to a moment called ego-desperation. It is a moment of admitting, "I cannot do it by myself." I must turn my life over to the enlightenment and empowerment of God as I understand him. I must ask God to make me a channel of his love, to fill my wells so that I can give the thirsty a drink from my supply.

When We Love, God Acts

This is the second of my statements about God and love. I think that I did not always believe that when we love, God acts. I do now. I used to think that our actions changed things. If I defended the truth, fed the hungry, shouted from the housetops what was whispered into my ear, it would change everything. The contagion of my truth, my compassion, and my virtue would eventually envelop the whole world. These were my thoughts during my "messianic period," the time when I was playing at being God. Now I believe much more simply that when we love, God's grace flows into this world through the channel of our love: healing it, straightening its twistedness, mending its brokenness, and enlightening its darkness. We are only God's instruments.

I am convinced that when you and I accept the grace of loving and we use it, we will be fulfilling the condition for God's action. Our love is the channel through which God's healing and helping grace will flow. Most of us do not have great talent, but we can all do small things with great love. And it is this that is essential. The loving mother who has her hands full of children, the silent monk who prays in some distant monastery, the old person whose vision is failing, the adolescent who worries about his acne—they are all capable of accepting and putting into practice the gift of love. And when they do, God will act. Because of those who love, God will change this world.

Can We Really Love Everyone? Even Our Enemies?

I remember once arguing my case for a life of love against fifteen others. They obviously did not believe what I did. I was really trying to swim upstream that night. My friends who were arguing against me were releasing their pent-up angers. It is so easy for most of us to get into an embattled siege mentality. We get sick of people lying to us, laundering their language, twisting the truth, and falsifying the facts. We want to hate them and to fight. My friends typified these urges. They cited one case after another—all hopeless types. Their conclusion: "You just can't love some people." Secretly, I think that they were confusing *like* with *love*. And I probably wasn't clear about my meaning of love, and the many faces of love.

For all our "fight or flight" tendencies, we are called to love. Despite all our petty squabbles, the towering figure of Christ stands over our lives and over all human history. He says, "Love only your friends? Why, even the heathens do this. I am asking you to love your enemies also." It is at moments like this that we face the difficult challenges and the consequences of a life of love. We slowly come to believe that this kind of love can only be a grace or gift of God. God could not ask us to love people we don't even like, unless he were willing to help us and to empower us. So we slowly come to believe that our love is a gift of God and at the same time the condition for his action. "This is all I command you. . . . I will do the rest."

The Big Question: Does Love Make Us Happy?

At the Last Supper, Jesus prepares to wash the feet of his Apostles. Of course Peter protests. I swear, the man they called the "Rock" always had footprints around his mouth. You see, a host washed the feet only of guests that the host wished to honor. After Peter's protest, "Oh no, you're not going to wash *my* feet," Jesus talks about the truth he was forever explaining and living. He makes it clear that every Christian must make his or her life an act of love. He acknowledges his lordship but insists that he did not come to be served but to serve. He explains to the Apostles the importance of seeing all authority as a service of love. Then Jesus turns to Peter: "If you don't get that, Peter, you don't get me. And if you don't get me, you just can't be my partner in the kingdom." So, with or without understanding, Peter urges Jesus to wash his head and hands, too.

In the Gospel of Saint John, Jesus concludes with this line:

> "Now that you know this truth, *how happy you will be* if you put it into practice!"   *John 13:17*

The happiness that can come only as a by-product to loving can be learned only by experiencing it. Such joy can only be described to the unloving, who will no doubt think of it as a fairy tale. A life that is an act of love can be presented only on a "Try it—you might like it" basis. But the alternative is clear. If a life of love is a fairy tale, the opposite is a nightmare.

Unloving people just don't care about anyone. They keep their grudges carefully labeled and stored in a memory bank. They don't trust others. And they feel safer behind an array of masks. They decide which one to wear depending on the occasion and the people present. They reason that walls are safer than bridges. Others have never passed their inspection tests. And the only people willing to enter into a relationship of sorts with them are just as cautious, just as phony, just as self-centered. It is a prison life. There are the cages with their bars. The loneliness can get very painful at times, but there are always distractions, like kicks and sensations. But then the unloving person can only ask, "What else is there?"

Love Is the Truth That Sets Us Free

I have told this story elsewhere and many times. It was one of those Copernican moments in my own life. And it has a definite point and place here. It was my personal discovery of the freeing effects of love.

I was the last speaker on a panel of three. I was very anxious to impress my audience, which was my own religious community. They had never heard me speak, and I wanted them to know what a gem was in their midst. I was "Fulton Sheen coming out from under wraps." I am rarely nervous before a speaking engagement. You see, I have a lot of mileage on my mouth. But on this night my mouth was dry and my hands were cold. I was nervous. So I prayed silently as I sat there waiting for my anticipated moment of glory. But my prayer brought no results. I was still nervous.

So I prayed again, reminding the Lord of his promise that whatever we asked in his name would be granted. But apparently not on that night. My mouth was still dry. My hands were still cold. Then I remembered the advice of an old spiritual sage. He said, "If you keep asking God the same question and you do not get an answer, try another question." So I asked God, "Why am I so nervous? And why won't you do anything about it? Are you trying to tell me something?"

Now, I have no difficulty believing in a loving God who interacts and communicates with us. In fact, this is the only God I do believe in. Anyway, on that night, sitting right there in front of 120 brother Jesuits, I know that God spoke to me. I know it was the grace of God. Somewhere, deep inside me, I heard:

> "You are getting ready to give another performance. And I don't need any more performances from you. Only acts of love. You want to perform for your brothers, so that they will know how good you are. They do not need that. They need you to love them, so that they will know how good they are."

I know I didn't invent that message. I know it was from God. It has profoundly changed me and changed my life. After I heard those words, I looked out at the members of my community. I looked at the aged who are retired from teaching and are preparing for the great retirement of death. Being rather young and vibrant, I asked myself, "What is it like to be old? What does it feel like when the traffic of life goes whizzing by? When no one ever stops to ask about you? What does that feel like?" Then I looked at those who are physically and chronically sick. They wake up every morning with an agony in their guts called an ulcer, or an ache in their bones called arthritis. Having enjoyed a lifetime of almost uninterrupted good health, I asked myself, "What is it like to feel sick almost all of the time? What is it like to take pain to bed with you at night and wake up with it in the morning?"

Then I looked at the four or five members of my community who are members of Alcoholics Anonymous. "What is it like?" I asked myself. "What is it like to live with an addiction? What is it like to struggle to maintain sobriety one day at a time? What is it like to stand up at a meeting and say, 'My name is _____, and I am an alcoholic'?" Then I looked at the men who are not very successful in their work. To be honest, God has blessed me with more success than I ever dreamed even in my most Technicolor dreams. "Do you feel like a failure?" I silently asked my less successful brothers. "Do you resent or envy the success of others? Do you ever wonder why everything seems to go wrong for you and right for others?"

Trying to walk for a mile in the shoes of another is not easy. It is the work of a virtue called empathy. Empathy is, I feel sure, the essential prelude to loving others. After my flood of empathic questions, I felt ashamed of my self-centered desire to impress these men. I had been praying for the grace to show them how good I was. I should have been praying for the grace to love them.

But God was not through with me that night. In another moment of grace, I remembered Mary Martin, the singer and entertainer. It was once said of her that "it would be difficult to sit in an audience of Mary Martin and to imagine that the audience loved her more than she loved the audience." Anyway, it was this Mary Martin who said that she never went out on any stage without first peeping through the stage curtains at her audience and whispering, "I love you! I love you! I love you!" Mary Martin maintains that you can't be nervous when you are truly loving. The only way to be nervous, she has said, is to be self-conscious. You can be nervous only if you are asking, "How am I doing?" But you can't be nervous when you are asking, "How are you doing?"

This last question breaks the fixation that most of us have with ourselves.

So I looked out at my community on that memorable evening, and under my breath I promised, "I don't know if I have really loved you before, but I am going to love you, love you, love you." Almost as if a magic wand had been waved over my head, all the nervousness and tension vanished. Saliva came back into my mouth, and blood flowed again into my fingertips.

It was a lesson I had learned before, and would have to learn again and again. Someday, perhaps, I will be fully open to its meaning. Love is a liberation. Love is the lubricant that makes life a lot easier. Love breaks the tense and nervous preoccupation with ourselves. It frees us for a life of peace. Love holds out to us the only substantial hope for lasting happiness.

Processing These Ideas about Love

1. *Write Your Own Version of "What Love Does" and "What Love Doesn't."* Make a list of things that you think love would include and exclude. Based on this list, what do you think love is asking you to do or to avoid doing?

2. *List and Compare.* Write the names of the ten people you know best. Then rank these *same* ten people according to their active capacity for loving. Put the most loving (in your judgment) at the top of the list and the least loving at the bottom. Then rank the *same* ten people according to their apparent happiness, peace, and contentment. Again, put the happiest (in your judgment) at the top of your list, the least happy at the bottom.

Now compare these two lists. What is your conclusion? Are the *happiest* people also the *most loving?* Does loving really make us happy? What do you think?

3. *Try an Exercise in Empathy.* Choose a family member or a close friend, and write what you think it is like to be that person. Include as many details as possible. Then present your description to the person chosen. Ask humbly, "Is this really what it's like to be you? Have I looked and listened well or poorly?"

4. *Write in a Journal.* Finally, record in a journal a short list of problems you have recently experienced. Include old and familiar worries, difficult people, physical or health problems, repugnant duties, and so forth. After each "problem" recall the power of this problem to attract your attention and to diminish your capacity for loving. Did you have much concern left over for others? How did you treat others while this problem was at its peak? What was going on inside you at this time?

Do the insights you have gained from this self-exploration help you to understand others in your life? Would you conclude that hurting, whether it is externally visible or invisible, diminishes the human capacity for loving?

Remember

Love is a poor mathematician. It does not keep a careful count of what it has done. It just goes on doing . . . and smiling.

We must stretch by stepping out of our comfort zones.

We are all pilgrims, beings in process. Each one of us must march bravely to a personal drummer, climb our personal mountains, struggle for a destiny that is ours alone. I am I and you are you. Sometimes it seems much safer just to follow the good old beaten path. It feels safer to be a member of a flock. The "road less traveled" always seems so risky. But we are all pilgrims, each on the way to a personal, private destiny. There is no "one road for all." We are each gifted with an enormous but unique potential. However, in our rendezvous with destiny, we have to take chances, run risks, get rejected and be hurt, be knocked down and get back up on our feet. We must learn to survive defeats. It is all so wild, so terrifying, so adventuresome.

Pilgrims on their way to a promised land, it would seem, have to be, above all, courageous and very tough. Sometimes it will feel as though determination alone compels us to go on. It is so tempting just to find a place in the sun and stay there. The fertile imagi-

nation can and will make up a thousand rationalizations: "That's just not me." "This is just as good." "Why try something new?" We can send out a thousand small distress signals. Bleeding hearts will surely see them and rush to our rescue. Our rescuers will also make excuses for us. They will assure us that they like us just as we are, that there is no need to try for something more.

So we are doomed to stay in the same place. We do the very same things we have always done. Our actions and reactions become very predictable. Some will call us dependable. Others will be able to see that we are paralyzed by our fears. We are stagnant and stifled. Each day becomes a carbon copy of the previous. Each year begins to look very much like the last one. Our bones ache a little more. New wrinkles mark our faces. There is less energy. But otherwise we are just the same person we have always been, living in a world without challenges or change.

A Definition of Terms

Each of us lives for the most part in the safe confines of a comfort zone. As long as we stay within that area, we feel secure and we know what to do. We are well practiced at the things inside the circle of this comfort zone. There are certain emotions we can easily express because we are comfortable expressing them. Others are just outside our comfort zone, and still others seem impossibly distant. Some actions come easily and comfortably. We can do them, as it were, with one hand behind our backs. But others tend to terrify us. We can break out in a rash just thinking about them. Our comfort zones even extend to the clothes we wear. We are comfortable wearing certain fashions and certain colors, but there are others in which we would feel too conspicuous or too plain and, therefore, ill at ease.

One of our obstacles to growth is that we tend to rationalize these comfort zones. Successful rationalization always begins with a laundering of our language. We must pick just the right words. So we say, "That's just not me." "That's not my style." "I would just not be comfortable doing that." The most successful rationalization is simply to say, "I just can't." It has a certain "finality" about it. If we were to say "I won't," others might ask us why. But when we say "I can't," people tend to leave us alone. If you can't, you just can't. Ah! Alone in my sweet comfort zone.

The deliberate stepping out of our comfort zones is what we mean by "stretching." Right at the top, however, a qualification should be made. We stretch when we try something that is *right and reasonable.* We don't undress in public or hurt or embarrass someone else just to stretch. Stretching challenges us to do something that seems right and reasonable, but from which we have always been inhibited by fear. For example, I would like to give a speech in public, or I would like to express my true feelings. However, I have always felt too intimidated to try it. This would be a good area in which to stretch.

Obviously, all growth involves some stretching. I have to attempt new things if I am to change. At first, I may feel clumsy, awkward, and more than a little self-conscious. But every time I try the same stretch, I will be a little more comfortable. Finally, what was once outside my comfort zone will now be within it. Repeated stretching will usher me into a new and larger world. I will be much more free. Eventually I will develop a "stretch mentality." I will actually enjoy trying new things. The old fears and crippling inhibitions that once painted me into a small corner of life will seem so stupid. I will even wonder why I ever let myself be terrorized by such toothless animals.

Stretching can be compared to being born. Have you ever seen a delivery? The newborn baby looks as though it would rather return to the warm womb from which it came. But the womb was in fact very confining. The baby had to be wherever its mother was. Now the baby has come into a new world, a larger world. With time and a little practice, the baby will be able to explore this bigger world. The person who is determined to stretch is by the force of that determination introduced into a larger world. Such a person can then explore that larger and more magnificent world. The cramping confines of a comfort zone gradually give way to the fullness of life and happiness.

Now we can obviously *think* our way into a new way of *acting*. For example, as I learn to think of myself as competent, I am empowered to attempt more and more difficult things. However, stretching involves a reverse process. Stretching means *acting* my way into a new way of *thinking*. For example, I don't think I can give a speech in public. My concept of myself does not include this ability. Somehow I just don't think that "I have it." Then one day I stretch. I give a speech, and everyone tells me how good it was. I gradually learn to think of myself as a speaker. I have acted my way into a new way of thinking about myself. All of us have had a similar experience, I think. Do you remember the first time you were able to swim without the support of another? "I can swim!" you shouted to the whole world. The same thing was true of the first cake you baked or the first time you hit a home run. You did something for the first time, and your concept of yourself changed. Previously, you were sure that you were a person who couldn't, and now you think of yourself as a person who can! Another victory for stretching.

Areas for Stretching

The possibilities are as large as the world a person wants to live in. But there are certain areas that for many of us seem to need special consideration. The first of these is *the expression of emotions.* It has been demonstrated again and again that the bottling up of our feelings inside us is self-destructive. We just can't get away with it. What we don't speak out we will act out. We will act out our unexpressed feelings on our own bodies by getting headaches or ulcers. We will act out our pent-up feelings on innocent third parties. Or we will pout or harbor a grudge that will gradually poison us. But we won't get away with the suppression of our feelings. We need to tell others how we truly feel. The penalty for refusal is unhappiness. The stretching in this area calls for the mature, the right and reasonable expression of our feelings. Please see the chapter on communication (practice 8) to learn the needed techniques for doing this. Or for a fuller study of the question, look at the appropriate guidelines proposed in *Will the Real Me Please Stand Up?* (Powell and Brady, Tabor Publishing, 1985).

A profitable area for stretching could be included under the title "Things I have always wanted to do but have been afraid to try." All of us have at some time dreamed about reaching for a star. But our fears, especially the fear of failure, have always restrained us. Of course, our fears are largely subjective and personal. What some of us fear to try, others may find very natural and easy. But let me include here some typical challenges: giving a speech, telling others how grateful we are, disagreeing with a teacher or a boss, going sailing, flying through the skies, learning a musical instrument, speaking up when silence would be so much easier, taking dancing lessons, writing a letter of praise or protest to a publication. What have you always wanted to do, but were afraid to try?

Certainly included in areas for stretching would be *personal authenticity,* or *realness.* Such authenticity calls for listening to what is going on inside us and in a mature way laying it on the line. If I am uncertain inside, then what I have to do is admit my uncertainty. If I don't understand something, then I must admit that I really don't understand it. When I know that I am gifted at doing something, and my talent is needed, then I must step forth and volunteer. I will, always in a mature way, make known my needs. I will not be afraid to ask favors from others. And if something hurts, I will say an audible "Ouch!" Eventually, I will be able to retire my repertoire of masks and pretenses. I will be honest and open and real! And I am nothing if not real. This is certainly a right and reasonable goal to set for myself.

An additional area for stretching would be *relationships.* Relationships are essential for a full and happy life. However, for many of us, starting a relationship is difficult. It would be a good place to stretch. This usually involves introducing oneself to another. "You look like a person I would like to know." Oh, gulp, we think. Well, do it anyway. A relationship also and eventually involves sharing "secrets" and doing things together. The stretching to initiate relationships challenges us to open up, to admit one's secrets, to extend invitations, to risk rejections, to take one's chances.

Of course, there are numerous "little stretches" that all of us should attempt. You know, the kinds that don't cost us much inner crunch or struggle. You are no doubt familiar with the saying "No pain, no gain." So you ask, "Why bother with these almost costless stretches?" It is true that these smaller stretches might seem insignificant. Still, if undertaken regularly, they nudge us out of our old, familiar grooves. And just that small movement can cause great ripples of change and growth. Little by little, we move from being a person who is trying to stretch to a stretching-type, adventurous person. Little by little, we find ourselves living in a much larger, more exciting world. We find ourselves living every moment as new and fresh.

Among the small stretches we might try would be these: Take a rainy day nap. Make an appointment with yourself to relax and reflect. Make a list of things to be done today, and stick to it. Do a favor for someone anonymously. Write a song or a poem. Sincerely compliment someone who never compliments you. Say no to a request without giving in to guilt feelings. Spend some time talking to a child. Hold someone's hand. Try something you might fail at. Go slow when you feel rushed. Give away something that you feel attached to. C'mon. Go for it!

It has been calculated by the students of human nature that the average person uses only 10 percent of his or her potential. Ninety percent of what might have been dies quietly of frustration by fear and inhibitions. Stretching works to improve these odds. Without stretching, we will forfeit 90 percent of life's beauty, goodness, and giftedness. We will go to our graves with 90 percent of our potential goodness and giftedness unused. Sad, eh? Ninety percent of our potential sealed into our coffins with our own mortal remains.

Stretching:
Reaching for the New,
Leaving the Old

Something that pays off quickly and rewards us immediately usually comes easily. Unfortunately, most stretching requires time and repetition. We usually don't kill the dragons of our fears with one stroke of the sword. However, if we stay with it, we will experience a growing sense of ease and peace in doing what we could never do before.

I have clear recollections of my own early shyness. But, fortunately for me, kind and loving people challenged me. So I got into debating, and I entered elocution and oratorical contests at school. I thought I might die or at least faint from embarrassment during my first appearances on the stage. But after a while and with perseverance, most of the shyness began to disappear. Now it is almost completely gone. (Every once in a while I experience a shy little kid somewhere deep down inside myself. He blinks and wants to know if all this is real.) But don't forget: Growth is always a gradual process, a bridge slowly crossed and not a corner sharply turned.

I remember reading about the liberation of the Nazi concentration camps by the Allied Forces at the end of World War II. It seems that many of the prisoners came hesitantly out of their prison barracks, blinked in the sunlight, and then slowly walked back into those barracks. It was the only life they had known for such a long time. They were accustomed to think of themselves as prisoners. They couldn't imagine themselves as free. So they weren't able to adapt immediately to acting like free human beings. I think that all of us somehow share this very human tendency. We have been imprisoned by our fears for such a long time. We go on living in a small but safe corner and, sadly, using only 10 percent of our giftedness. Then we are challenged to stretch— to take the first awkward steps out of our own personal prisons. We blink in the sunlight and want to go back silently to the things we have known, to our cramped but familiar comfort zones.

One of the relentless laws of our humanity is that when we give up one pleasure, we must be consoled by a new and, if possible, a greater pleasure. Human nature abhors a vacuum. The pleasure we give up in stretching is safety. We are stepping out over the fences and ditches of our inhibitions; we are leaving our "place in the sun." We are giving up the security of our comfort zones. Those comfort zones have always offered us an unchallenged and unchallenging existence. The substitute pleasure in stretching is freedom. We are becoming free. We are acting against our crippling fears, and this is liberating. Before stretching, we were using only 10 percent of our giftedness—the giftedness of our senses, emotions, minds, and hearts. By stretching, we are slowly coming out of our darkness into the light, out of our loneliness into love, out of our partial living into the fullness of life.

It is true, I am sure, that there is no such thing as a strong or weak will. What is strong or weak in us is *motivation.* Motivation sets our wills into action. It is the fuel of desire that moves us. Obviously, the motivation to stretch will somehow relate to our increased freedom, enjoyment, and self-actualization. All of us desire the sure and certain rewards of a fuller life and greater freedom. As we proceed to stretch, this motive becomes stronger and stronger.

Motivating Underachievers

In every school there is a group called the underachievers. They have all that is needed except the drive or incentive to use their gifts. And in almost every school there is a class or course for these underachievers. One thing is almost always suggested in these classes: "Do something on your own. Try to stimulate your own interest. Read a book. Volunteer to do a project." Most underachievers sit on the fringe of a class, waiting for the teacher to inspire them. But three out of four teachers are simply not inspiring. It's the law of averages. The classic underachiever gets used to sitting on the curbstones of life, having one identity crisis after another. He or she keeps mumbling, "Who am I? What am I worth?

Who cares anyway?" It's like sitting in a rocker. It doesn't get you anywhere, but it gives you something to do.

Until the underachiever is persuaded to stretch, this limbo of a half existence will go on. But with stretching, the underachiever will experience an enthusiasm that will build on itself. When we become involved in something, our very activity generates further enthusiasm. And enthusiasm feeds on itself. It naturally increases and multiplies. Stretching overcomes our inertia, and from there on we gradually become self-motivating.

Processing These Ideas about Stretching

We have already talked about profitable areas for stretching. To be more specific, try one of the following "stretches" every day. Take them in order until you have completed the list. Then start repeating. See for yourself how these stretches will release you from the small and lonely world of comfort zones. Experience the liberation of acting against your fears and painful inhibitions. Remember: one a day, and one stretch at a time.

1. An emotion I have never shared. I will share that emotion today.
2. A risk I have never taken. Today I will take that risk.
3. An achievement I have never tried. Today I will try for that achievement.
4. A rejection I have never chanced. Today I will take that chance.
5. A need I have never admitted to anyone. Today I am going to admit that need.
6. An apology I have never been able to make. Today I will make that apology.
7. An affirmation I have never offered. Today I am going to offer that affirmation.
8. A secret I have never shared. Today I will share it with someone.

9. A hurt I have never revealed. Today I will reveal that hurt.
10. A love I have never expressed. Today I am going to tell some-one "I love you."

Remember

A larger world and a fuller life await you.
But you have to grow into it by stretching.
C'mon. Go for it! Make your day!

We must learn to be "goodfinders."

In one sense most human searches are a success. We all seem to find whatever it is we are looking for. The object of our expectations seems to have been there all the time, waiting to be discovered by us. From childhood on, some of us seem to be braced for disappointment. Of course, we then find disappointments in abundance. Life becomes a scenario of broken dreams and disillusion. Our heroes always seem to collapse and reveal feet of clay. What can go wrong, does go wrong. After wandering through all the trials of life, we find that the road is a dead end.

Others of us have been guided by a different compass. We seem to be moving along the high road. The scenery is beautiful, and the people along the way are very helpful. We seem to be surrounded by goodness and good fortune. There are a few dark days here or there, but in the end everything seems to work out well. We know by personal experience what the Lord God meant when he looked upon his creation and beamed: "It is very good!"

The Common Denominator
of Happiness

A few years ago some researchers decided to study the success of happiness in a purely scientific way. So they sought out the 100 most successful and contented people they could find. Then they went to work interviewing these 100 blessed souls. All information gleaned from these interviews was dutifully and carefully fed into a giant computer. The hope was to discover what all these people might have in common. The scientific interviewers were seeking to find the common denominator of human happiness.

At first the scientific search for this common denominator proved to be quite discouraging. These most successful and contented people did not seem to have anything in common—certainly not education or background. Some were grade school dropouts, while others had received doctorate degrees. Some had come from wealth, while others had to rise above the poverty into which they were born. Of all the categories, the nearest thing to a common denominator was that 70 of the 100 persons interviewed had come from small towns, population under 15,000. However, in the final tally of all the information in the computer, the search was rewarded with success. In fact, it ended in a blaze of satisfied discovery. The scientists found that each and every one of the 100 subjects was a . . . well, was a "goodfinder." However, the word *goodfinder* had to be invented to describe this common trait.

Definition of a Goodfinder

By definition, a goodfinder is one who looks for and finds what is good in him or herself, in others, and in all the situations of life. It is probably true that we usually do find whatever we are looking for. If we set ourselves to find evil, there is plenty of it to be discovered. On the other hand, if we seek to find goodness, there is also much goodness waiting for our discovery. If we look for imperfections in ourselves and in others, the search will no doubt be successful. However, if we look beyond the weak and the foolish things and seek to find the good and beautiful things that no one else had ever looked quite far enough to find, our search will be rewarded with success. It all depends upon what we are looking for. "Two men looked out from prison bars. / One saw mud and one saw stars."

An old country preacher once exclaimed, "People are always trying to explain the problem of evil. Well, there certainly is a lot of evil to be explained. But there is another problem. How can we explain all the goodness in this world?" The preacher was right, I think. How can we explain the people who are faithful in keeping their promises? How do we explain human devotion and caring, a life spent in the service of others? How do we explain heroism? There is a lot of goodness, and often it is found in unlikely persons and places.

We do find whatever we are looking for. I have tried to imagine what would happen if a priest, a poet, and a politician were to walk down the same street together. They would each look for and find something different. The priest might think about all the souls in the high rises, and wonder about their lives and what God is doing in those lives. He might ask difficult questions about the providence of God. The poet has meanwhile been absorbed with the beauty of the overhanging branches, a veritable tunnel of trees. He sees the nuances of shades, exults in the riot of colors. He walks down the street in rapture. The politician's eyes scan the same high rises, and he mentally calculates, "There are a lot of votes up there." He wonders about who the ward leader is, and whether or not someone is trying to register all these voters. The priest, the poet, and the politician all look for and find something different in the very same experience.

Looking for the Good in Myself

You will remember the exercise called "the empty chair fantasy." It was used to process the ideas proposed under practice 1. In a workshop on attitudes that I once presented, I gave this fantasy exercise to the participants. A year later, I got the following letter:

> Your flyer advertised for emotionally stable people, but I sneaked in. I have been a psychological mess for most of my twenty-nine years. However, after that "empty chair fantasy," I knew my troubles were over. The "me" who came out to sit in that chair was a battered wimp. She looked like a beaten puppy who was bracing for more abuse. The sad part is that I knew who had administered those beatings. I had. I had demoralized myself completely with constant criticism. Whenever I looked into a mirror, I did not look for the beautiful smile, the straight white teeth, or the flashing eyes. I looked for (until I found it) the zit, the ugly pimple. Whenever I wrote something, I would look for a misspelled or misused word. I had succeeded brilliantly in destroying my own self-image. When we got to say one thing to our imagined self in your exercise, I could only apologize to myself. "Hey, I'm really sorry. I'm sorry for what I have done to you. And I solemnly promise: From now on I am going to be a friend to you. I am going to support and affirm you. I'm going to praise and appreciate you. I'm going to notice the good things in you. I promise you: I'm really going to try."
>
> It's a year later now. I have been true to the promises I made to myself. And every day I become more certain that my troubles are over. I have terminated with my psychotherapist. He agreed that I didn't need him anymore, at least for now. It has been like the beginning of a new life, like a second chance at living. I have become a friend to myself. I have begun to focus on the good things in myself. It has made all the difference. At last I am a reasonably happy and healthy person.

Looking for what is good in ourselves is not in any way conceit or vanity. It can and should conclude with a humble act of gratitude. Looking for the good in myself is the only reasonable thing to do if I want to be happy. Bernard of Clairvaux once said that the perfect expression of true humility in the New Testament was the Magnificat of Mary, the mother of Jesus. In it, you will remember, Mary proclaims to her cousin, Elizabeth, that she is very happy: "My spirit rejoices in God my Savior. From this day on, everyone who really knows me will also know how blessed I have been." Humility doesn't deny but rejoices in the gifts of God. Humility is grateful for its blessings.

To be a true goodfinder, I must set my own sights on the many gifts of God to me. I should slowly make a "lover's count" of my blessings. I should look for and find all the goodness and the giftedness with which the Lord has blessed me. I must face the obvious fact that whatever I have is God's gift to me. I should be happily grateful for these gifts that are a part of me.

Looking for What Is Good in Others

People are something like wildflowers. Their goodness and beauty can be so easily missed or taken for granted. Sometime everyone should pick a wildflower and study it carefully. There are delicate veins in its leaves. The petals are so fragile, the blossom so beautiful. If you do this, turn the flower in the sunlight and look for its special symmetry. It has a beauty all its own.

In the words of Roy Croft, "I love you . . . for passing over all the foolish, weak things that you can't help dimly seeing in me, and for drawing out into the light all the beautiful belongings that no one else had looked quite far enough to find."

People, too, need a closer look. But we do have to look beyond the weak and foolish things that cover the goodness in most of us. We must go in search of the beauty that no one else has ever looked long enough or far enough to discover. However, let all goodfinders be forewarned: Others will think of you as naive or Pollyannaish. The world at large cannot easily believe in the optimism of goodfinders.

It has often occurred to me that the function of a crisis in a human relationship is really a challenge. Most people in such a relationship seem to go along for a while on a plateau of peace. Then there is the storm or the silence of a crisis. Maybe it all starts with the fear of intimacy or with simple boredom. Or it could be that there is a win-lose rhythm, a struggle for dominance. Whatever its cause and nature, there arises a *crisis*. As the Chinese say, it is both a danger and an opportunity.

Most crises are a warning signal, I think. The crisis is signaling the partners to find each other at a deeper level of discovery. You may well have experienced this at some time in your life. Do you remember a time when you felt estranged from someone close to you? You wondered if love was over. There were angry words, wounded feelings, and a long, smoldering resentment. Then you got sudden word that the other person was seriously sick or badly hurt. All the surface conflict and consequent estrangement seemed to vanish. You rushed to the side of the other person. You poured out parts of your own depths that you didn't know existed. A new and deeper bond was forged in that moment. The tinsel of shallow love mellowed into gold. You had found each other at a deeper level. It was a new beginning in the relationship.

Finding Good in
All the Situations of Life

It has been said that our biggest opportunities will probably come into our lives disguised as problems. Problems have a way of challenging us, of calling out of us coping capacities of which we were unaware. Problems can jolt us out of our predictable routines but only to introduce us to a life of new possibilities. In the end, we probably profit more from suffering than we do from success. But I feel sure that the extent of benefits derived is determined by our habitual mind-set. We must be ready to look for and find good in all the situations of life.

Recently I heard that a friend of mine was arrested for a minor traffic violation. This woman is the mother of five children, and a very dear and gentle person. At any rate, she was driving to a department store in a suburb of Chicago. A large and overserious policeman stalked into the store after her and demanded to see her driver's license. He said that she had made an improper turn before arriving at the store. When she asked him to tell her that he was only joking, he (honestly) arrested her. While he was handcuffing her, he swung her arm around behind her. It struck him, and so he added the charge: "Striking an officer." Then, believe it or not, he called for backup help. My friend was taken to the police station, strip-searched, fingerprinted, and put into a cell.

I had heard all these details before I actually saw my friend. When I told the story to a lawyer friend, he gasped, "This is a lawyer's dream. It has a 'quick million' written all over it." He wanted to know if the woman in question had a lawyer.

Then I had a chance to hear the whole story again, firsthand. My friend assured me that "it was one of the most meaningful experiences of my whole life. I told the officers that I finally understood how Jesus must have felt. I assured them that during the week before Easter when we recall his suffering, I would be much more understanding than ever before. They kept insisting, 'We're only doing our duty, Ma'am.' And I kept reassuring and thanking them."

By the way, I did ask her if she intended to file a lawsuit against the suburb or maybe against the arresting officer. She replied, "Oh, no. The arresting officer was just a poor boy who overreacted. Do you know, he kept calling me 'Ma'am,' but once he slipped and said 'Mom.' Somehow I'm sure he was just looking for a mother."

We speak of having to "reframe" our difficult experiences in order to find the good in them. I suppose that the term comes from the reframing of a painting. The frame brings out certain details that might otherwise have been missed. When we reframe an experience, we go back over it to look for the silver lining in the dark cloud, to focus on the lessons learned, the advantages derived. Many psychotherapists ask their clients to repeat a story of misfortune. Only in the repetition, the client is asked to tell the same story as one of opportunity and profit. For example, James Whistler, the painter, wanted to be a career soldier until he flunked out of West Point. He was so depressed by his failure that he took up painting as therapy. The singer Julio Iglesias wanted only to be a soccer player until he was hurt and temporarily paralyzed. A nurse brought him a guitar to help him pass the time. It almost seems that when one door is closed, another is opened. The important thing is to be a goodfinder.

God, the Ultimate Goodfinder

At the time of Jesus, the world was a cold and cruel world. The rich spent their idle time in endless orgies, the poor lived in a grinding poverty. Two-thirds of all the people in that world were living in a subhuman form of slavery. The favorite sport of that world was watching two gladiators fight until one of them was fallen with wounds or exhaustion. At this point the victorious gladiator would look to the spectators for further instructions. The spectators would then hold money or jewels in one hand, and with the thumb of the other point upward or down. The upthrusted thumb meant, "This money or these jewels are yours if you spare him. He was a vicious competitor and will come back to entertain us again." The down-pointing thumb was a signal that urged the victor, "Kill him. He was uninteresting. Put your sword through his throat."

Historians of the time tell us that when the victorious gladiator would transfix his fallen victim, there would arise a shout of celebration that would rock the whole city. It was as though a home run had been hit in a major-league baseball park during a World Series.

This was the world of which the Scriptures say: "God so loved the world that he sent his only begotten Son into the world, so that anyone who would believe in him would not die but would have eternal life. God sent his Son into the world not to judge or condemn it, but to love it into life" (John 3:16-17). The coming of Jesus into this world was the supreme act of goodfinding. The world that God found "very good" at creation was, for all its misery, still very good. Deep down inside every human heart, God resides and recognizes the goodness and giftedness that lies buried there.

We who are made in the image and likeness of God will share in God's happiness to the extent that we become goodfinders. There is even scientific, computerized proof for this.

Processing These Ideas about Goodfinding

1. *Journalize about Self.* Write several paragraphs describing your own three best qualities. Let it be the beginning of a lover's count of personal blessings.

2. *Journalize about Another.* Write a second set of paragraphs describing the three best qualities of someone you don't like.

3. *Reframe a Recent Experience of Crisis in Your Life.* Tell a friend or confidant the story of a recent trauma or disappointment, but in the context of opportunity and advantage. Recall the things you learned from the experience. Go over it and describe the good results, the profit derived from this experience.

Remember

Many of life's greatest opportunities come into our lives disguised as problems.

We must seek growth, not perfection.

It all seemed so noble, so generous, and if I say so myself, it even seemed so saintly: "Reach for the top. Give it your best. Don't settle for your second best." The very rhetoric of my zeal to do my best, to be my best, sent fire surging through my veins. But the rhetoric betrayed reality. The rhetoric was unrealistic. Nothing is ever perfect. My best was always flawed. The results of my zeal for perfection left a thick and bitter taste in my mouth. Deep inside me was a soft and long moan: "But I tried so hard. I gave it all I had. It was my best shot." Then I pounded my fists of frustration on the earth. I waved them at the sky. But it did no good. I was left to admit that I am imperfect. I am a mistake maker. The human condition of trial and error is my condition. I have tried all my cover-ups, my denials. I have tried to look as though I had it all together. But under all my sham and pretense, I knew all along that I could never match my dreams with my performance. I could never be perfect.

The Roots of Perfectionism

"Obsessive-compulsive" is a double-barreled diagnosis of trouble: trouble behind and trouble ahead. "Obsessive" has to do with the mind. An obsessive person thinks and rethinks almost constantly about the obsession, whatever it is. "Compulsive" refers to conduct or "doing." The compulsive person has to do, do, do. A compulsive person may wash his or her hands twenty times a day.

Now the fact is that some of us are obsessive-compulsive about perfection. And I would think that there is some of this in most of us. Even those who insist that they are not perfectionists are uncomfortable with being "mistake makers." They can recite chapter and verse of their willingness to be imperfect, but the recitation ends when they make a mistake. The extent to which we experience and act on this obsession and compulsion is the extent to which we are bound to suffer. It is not at all surprising to learn that perfectionists actually have the highest rate of depression among all human beings.

Like all of our tendencies, perfectionism has deeper, unexposed roots. Sometimes it betrays a hidden fear. For example, I may be thinking in an unconscious way, "If I am imperfect, people won't trust me" or "I won't ever be able to get ahead." Or there may be some all-or-nothing logic hiding beneath my surface thoughts: "If I am not perfect, then I am a failure." Sometimes, I secretly think (but rarely admit) that "if I am a failure, people will criticize me." Or it may be that a little voice from my past will ask in a whisper, "If I do not do a perfect job, what will Mommy or Daddy say?" It may well be that my drivenness for perfection is simply my way to get approval. And it may have started in early childhood, with Mommy and Daddy.

Early on in life, many of us get programmed to think this way. It may be that the message was acted out by exacting parents. They programmed us to be perfectionists by trying to be perfect themselves. Or it may be that the inclination to perfectionism was drilled into us by others who wanted to enjoy our performances vicariously. Peer pressure can be another strong factor. Many of us have had the experience of being laughed at. Afterward we secretly resolved never again to make a public mistake. The penalties are simply too painful, too embarrassing. If I am a "driven" person, someone has somehow placed expectations on me that can only become painful. Of course, it may have been a matter of my misinterpretation. But anyway, it is not what is said but rather what is heard that influences people, people like you and me.

The High Price of Perfectionism

Perfectionism always has a downward spiral. It leaves us room only for failure. Nothing ever comes off exactly as we planned it. And the end result of such failure is discouragement. Very often our frustrated hopes degenerate gradually into a disappointed anger. We act out our discouragement or anger in obnoxious ways, but they are always buried in pretense. Others would never suspect.

This self-destructive course of striving for perfection has been repeated in many lives. A young woman I met years ago admitted to me at our first meeting that she had twice tried suicide. However, she assured me that her nursing degree would definitely fill her painful sense of emptiness. Of course, she got the R.N. degree, but she was just as unhappy as before. By that time she was sure that marriage was all that she needed. A fine young man soon appeared on the scene, and they were married. But the depression that had haunted her all her life soon reappeared like a cloud over her head. At this time she was certain that children would be all that she needed. They would definitely make her happy. Soon enough she was the mother of three children. But the clear skies didn't last. It wasn't long before she was tearfully confiding in me that her children hated her. In fact, she said, her adolescent son was physically abusive to her. I urged her to seek family counseling to find out what her children were acting out. I don't think she ever accepted this suggestion.

Then a few years ago I got a long-distance phone call from her husband. "Jean is dead," he told me. "And the really sad news is that she killed herself. She drove our car into the garage and left the motor running while she waited to die. She left a suicide note on the kitchen table. In her last words to us, she said simply: 'Don't be sad. You tried.' " Jean was being waked at the time of our phone conversation. In fact, her husband was calling from the funeral home. I almost couldn't believe the objectivity in his bereavement. He knew of the occasional phone calls between Jean and me. He asked, "Did she ever mention to you that our children hated her?" "Yes," I admitted, "she did tell me that."

"Well, they did. In fact, at her wake in the next room, I can sense the relief in our children that she is gone." He continued: "She had all the goodwill in the world. She tried everything to distract herself from her pain. But she never really acknowledged the real source of that pain. She was a perfectionist. She had declared an all-out war on all forms of imperfection. She sought an unconditional surrender from the less than perfect. She hounded the children until they hated her. At least they hated the sound of her voice and the finger she pointed at them. She drove herself to physical and emotional exhaustion. It lasted for thirty-nine years. Then she died, with the simple farewell: 'Don't be sad. You tried.' "

The poor man admitted that he felt very sorry for her. But he added that he also felt sorry for all those other people out there "trying to wage war with the same demon of perfectionism. They die inch by inch, day by day. And even when they never really die, as my Jeannie, they lose all zest for living. They crawl into a corner of hopelessness, and there they wait for death to say 'It's over!' " Perfectionism is indeed a suicide course.

Denial of the Demon

Most of the people I know are reluctant to admit that the demon of perfectionism has dominated them. They remember some habit of slovenliness that seems to disqualify them. Yet, these same people are uncomfortable with personal mistakes or oversights. I admit that I am myself uncomfortable, even though I am not a full-fledged perfectionist. We semiperfectionists are impatient with the mistakes and oversights of others as well as our own. We find it hard to laugh at the mistakes and weaknesses of ourselves and others. We do not comfortably accept ourselves as trial-and-error types, and we are slow to concede this privilege to others. It may not be the most virulent form of perfectionism, but it is enough to diminish the joy of living for ourselves and for those around us.

Of course, any form or degree of perfectionism is unrealistic. And somehow it seems that denial itself is a symptom of the disease. Once we admit that perfectionism is obsessive-compulsive behavior, we have implicitly said that perfectionism is itself a form of imperfection, the very thing we cannot live with. Obviously, a real perfectionist cannot admit that unrealistic hopes or expectations bedevil him or herself. That would blow one's cover.

The Anatomy of Perfectionism

Perfectionism is humanly unhealthy. And the difference between one who is healthy and the perfectionist is that the healthy person is in control of his or her life. The perfectionist is controlled, is driven by a compulsion. The healthy person is free and chooses freely. The perfectionist is not free. He or she has to . . . must . . . should succeed, be perfect. It is a bondage, an imprisonment of the free spirit.

Perfectionism begins with a *belief.* Perfectionists believe that their worth is measured by their performance. Of course, mistakes then detract from personal worth. They also believe that the only way to impress others is by being perfect. In a sense they see themselves as solo performers. They are not part of a team but contestants on their own. The obvious *emotions* that result are fear and panic. Perfectionists fear the displeasure and the punishment of others. They know that somehow they will have to pay for possible imperfections. They will surrender the respect of others. And so the emotional groundswell results in a loneliness, sadness, and depression.

Because emotions by their nature are partly physical, there are *physical symptoms* of perfectionism. These will vary with the perfectionist and the "target organ" of the perfectionist. But there will be symptoms of stress that will probably affect sleeping and eating, and will produce tension. As a result of all these, there is a type of *behavior* by which perfectionists reinforce the original belief that started everything. Perfectionists are people pleasers, and so they work hard to meet the expectations of others. They overpromise themselves. They set unrealistic standards and have unrealistic expectations. They do not like to ask for help, because this would be a concession. It would be an admission of inadequacy.

Perfectionists believe that they will be accepted by others on the basis of their achievements. They think of themselves as successful if they do well, not by simply being who they are. Performance and responsibility are always more important than feelings or needs. The penalty for failure is a withdrawal of the love of others and the loss of self-esteem.

Perfectionists do not give themselves unconditional acceptance nor do they expect it from others. They do not give themselves permission to fail, so they are anxious and nervous before every performance. They do not think of others as supporting and encouraging them. They see others only as watching and ready with pen and paper to grade them.

Peaceful Acceptance of the Human Condition

Of course, there can be no reversal or healing of this obsession with perfection unless one becomes aware of the condition and the bondage that results. Perfectionism is indeed a slave master. To put one's happiness in the hands of such a master is indeed foolish. The human condition is that of weakness. We are all trial-and-error types, real mistake makers. Brute animals and fowls have been endowed with perfect instincts. They do their thing even for the first time as if guided by a built-in set of instructions. The white-tufted sparrow always builds its recognizable nest perfectly, even the first time. But we poor humans, endowed as we are with very limited instincts and the precious gift of intelligence, have to proceed by trial and error. We are prone to miscalculation. Our maturation process is a process. Our finest minds design a space capsule that explodes in space. Our best trains derail. Our airplanes crash. Our automobiles are recalled because of potentially fatal defects.

It is true that the human spirit has put a man on the moon and built high rises that soar to dizzying heights. But for every such success there are a thousand failures. For every experiment that succeeds, a litter of failures lie on the laboratory floor. However, we continue our corporate efforts to improve. At the same time, to deny the truth of the human condition is to invite pain and frustration into our lives.

Human blessedness in this matter requires us to face and accept the truth. We are error prone. We learn by trial and error. Failure is never ultimate and absolute failure. It is only a learning experience. *The only real failure is the one from which we learn nothing.* All failure can be educational. The truth that confession is good for the soul extends to this admission of our own folly and fragility. According to the old proverb already quoted, if and when we learn to laugh at ourselves, we shall never cease to be entertained. The possibilities are infinite.

A corollary of this basic truth is that we are collaborators and not competitors. We are all in this together. Each of us should learn from the experience of others. You don't have to rerun my failed experiments. It's all part of the sage advice: "Learn from the mistakes of others. You won't have time to make them all yourself." When Henry Ford produced the first Model T, he must have known that others would improve on his design and structure. Each generation surpasses the previous, but only because it stands on the shoulders of that previous generation.

Seeking Growth

If perfection is a torturous ideal, growth is not. Growth sees life as a process during which skills are gradually developed. Learning to play the piano starts with laboriously fingering the scales over and over again. Then we proceed to melodies, and these melodies become more and more "classical" as our proficiency develops. If perfectionism seeks to arrive immediately (if not sooner), growth knows that even the journey of a thousand miles begins with a single step. Time and practice are of the essence. Actually, once we get the knack, gradual growth is much more fun than instant arrival.

What would you say if I were to propose to you this choice: You come to two doors. One is marked "instant perfection" and the other is marked "gradual growth." Which door would you prefer to go through? Surprisingly, very few, in my own experience, have chosen "instant perfection." If they go through that door, it's all over. What do you do for an encore to perfection? The journey has come to an end. If one chooses, however, to go through the door of "gradual growth," such a person will experience the joy of getting better and better, and the process will be ongoing for a lifetime. There will be the little successes of growth, without the big failure of perfectionism.

A good way to choose growth is to set out to *enjoy* rather than to achieve perfection. As I write these words for the first time, I am trying to follow my own advice. Something in me knows that there must be a better way to say all this. There may even be a perfect way. But I do not write seven or eight drafts and tear them all up in despair because they are not perfect. I rather try to enjoy this sharing with you. I read over what I have written, cross out this or that, add a word here or there. Then I think, "There. That's pretty clear. Somehow I seem to have said it better than in my previous attempts. Maybe, just maybe, what I write will help someone." That's a consoling thought.

And here is the surprise bonus. If you set out to *enjoy,* you will actually do a better job than if you are determined to make it perfect. (Maybe you don't believe that yet, but I think that someday you will.) If you are in school, set the dials of your mind to enjoy the courses you are taking as much as you can. I'll bet the results will surprise you. If you hold a job, try to do your work with as much enjoyment as possible. You'll most likely notice an improvement in your performance. Setting out to achieve perfection, by contrast, will become stressful and demoralizing. The end result will probably be discouragement. And discouragement always wants to quit, to give it all up.

Some Antidotes for Perfectionism

1. With any obsessive-compulsive habit, it helps to distract yourself from it. So the next time you find yourself grinding your teeth trying to be perfect, direct all your thoughts to enjoying whatever it is you are doing. Be happy instead of hyper. This will create a new route for your brain waves. Such distraction from or defusing of the perfection mind-set will be telling your obsessive compulsion, "You don't own me. I declare myself free from your tyranny. I am my own person, not your slave." The same declaration of personal independence can be achieved by putting a time delay on my compulsion. If I think I've got to do it right now, let it wait for an hour or even a day.

2. Desensitize yourself to the failures of imperfection. Talk over, laugh at, be open about your failures or imperfections. In this way you will eventually learn to be more comfortable with the human condition. You will also find, I am sure, that others will like you more. They will be able to identify with you. Many of us have somehow come to believe that others are impressed by our perfect performances. We think that they expect us to be perfect. So we try to look good, even when we aren't. The fact of the matter is that others, who experience the same human condition of weakness, would feel greater kinship if they knew that we are fragile and foolish, too. Admit it, and the world will applaud.

Processing These Ideas about Perfectionism

1. *Make Two Lists.* On one of these lists, enumerate the advantages of perfectionism, and on the other, the disadvantages.

2. *Journalize to Get in Touch with Yourself.* Write in a stream-of-consciousness way about yourself. In what do you believe your worth consists? Do you ever experience the emotions and physical symptoms of a perfectionist? Are you aware of an inordinate focus on yourself, on your performance, your mistakes, your aloneness? What would you be forfeiting if you failed in an important matter? What is the worst thing that could happen if you were to fail?

3. *Make a List.* Name all of the skills you have gradually and joyfully acquired, for example, playing a musical instrument; playing a game like golf, tennis, or soccer; learning to cook or bake. Recall that it was a process and that you were not an instant success.

4. *Write in a Journal.* Write about yourself as a person seeking growth rather than perfection. Whether you are a student, a homemaker, a salesperson, or whatever else, describe yourself in the posture of growing rather than being perfect. Would growth be preferable and profitable for you? Put down in writing the pros and cons.

Remember

Failures are just learning experiences. The only real failure is the one from which we have learned nothing.

We must learn to communicate effectively.

The human condition has been compared to a person trapped at the bottom of a deep dry well. All calls for help go unanswered. They seem to be blown away by the winds that howl at the top of the well. Hope begins to wear thin. Then, when hope seems certainly to be on its deathbed, an answering call comes from the top of the well: "We know that you are down there. We are coming with help. We will rescue you." There is an explosion of joy in the heart of the trapped person. "Thank God, someone finally knows that I am here!"

It is like this in real communication. The person who has opened up to another and has been heard no doubt feels the same sense of relief and exhilaration. "Thank God, someone finally knows what it is like to be me."

"We Are As Sick As We Are Secret"

The secrets that we keep hidden inside us become the poison that makes us sick. Eventually these secrets will destroy us. Poet laureate John Berryman, who leaped to his death from a bridge, wrote the line: "We are as sick as we are secret." He alone knew what private demons drove him to his death. But the words he left behind, his life, and his death are a legacy of warning to the rest of us. By a strange kind of human internal fermentation, what we keep inside us turns to poison. Still, most of us go on sheltering our fatal secrets because we don't want to run the risk of rejection, ridicule, or condemnation.

Inside us, in the sealed vaults of our privacy, our secrets seem like smoke. Whatever I am afraid to share spreads out until I am not sure what it really is, where it begins, and where it ends. If only I could put it all out, like pieces of a jigsaw puzzle, it might make sense. It is so true that the first obstacle to communication is really inside each of us. *I cannot tell you what I am not telling even myself.* And somehow, even if I could find the courage to open up, I'm not sure what I would say.

A good place to start, of course, would be to get in touch with the fears that haunt and imprison me. What would happen if I started peeling off the layers of my pretense and exposed my hiddenness to the light of day? What if I were to tell other human beings what it is like to be me? Would they understand? A thousand questions and doubts come to haunt me. Would I lose my reputation? Would others laugh at or reject me? Would I somehow be punished for my honesty? Would they use it against me at some later time? Would they be shocked to know? Would I be accused of lying? Of course I have been a phony, but would others say it bluntly? I get lost in all my questions and doubts. Somehow I recognize reality in all of them. Meanwhile, I go on with my pretense, hoping that I will get through one more day undetected. I cave in to the peer pressure. I take my cues from others. I find a mask to wear, a way to exist in this frightening world.

Communication

Communication is a nice word. Everybody seems to be for it, just as they are for love and peace. Communication has been called the lifeline of love. In its root meaning, it refers to an act of sharing. It implies that two or more persons now have something "in common" because it has been shared. In its most profound sense, communication is a sharing of the persons themselves. By our ongoing communication, you get to know me, and I get to know you. We have this in common: ourselves. Of course, it is not always a smooth and painless thing, this communication. If you are to know me, I must be willing to share with you the hidden angers that seethe somewhere in my depths. I must tell you about the humiliating fears that seem to diminish my stature. At times, too, the green head of envy will rise up between us. I will be tempted to get into a win-lose struggle for domination with you. Somehow I must be sure that you are as committed to honest and open communication as I am. I don't want you to use my openness as a pretext to scorn me or leave me. And I must be ready to guarantee that your openness will never be abused by me. And I must be ready to put aside my own agendas to listen to you, to find out what it is like to be you.

The Fears of Intimacy

If we do really commit ourselves to communication, intimacy between us is inevitable. Everyone has some fear of intimacy, and so everyone instinctively fears communication for this reason. One of the problems is that our fears are as unique as our fingerprints. Your fear of intimacy has a different shading than mine. Some of us fear *separation.* "I don't want to get too close to you because afterward you might leave me. You might die or divorce me. It is safer 'not to love than to lose.' " Others of us fear *fusion.* "If I share everything with you, what will be left for me? Will I still have my own turf, the place where I can be alone? I don't want to be like a glob of wax melted into one larger glob. I hate symbiotic relationships in which you don't know where one person ends and the other begins. That's enmeshment, not intimacy."

Still others of us fear *rejection*. "If you really get to know me, you won't like me. You will gradually lose interest once you find out all you want to know. You will find a pretext or occasion to move on to someone else." My own personal fear seems to be a fear of *responsibility*. If I get too close to another, I will feel obliged to be there for that person in his or her moments of need. But I almost always feel overextended, overinvolved. And I don't want to overpromise myself. In addition to this, I also feel a serious aversion for exposing the weak, the hurting, the wounded parts of me. My act, or role, has always been to look like I have it all together. It is very difficult for me to reveal my total self. I don't want people to know what a fraction I am. It is the bag and baggage of my perfectionism.

Very often people, for their own reasons, head off intimacy before it can grow deep roots. An argument, sulking or pouting, carrying a grudge, or assigning someone to the "doghouse" are all excellent inhibitors of intimacy. Perhaps the main problem with this ploy is that it can convince even its perpetrators. We don't admit, even to ourselves, that intimacy is the real issue. We cover over our fear with the "sincere pretense" of anger or resentment. It does keep others at a distance. No one can really get close to a porcupine, right? What we really fear, of course, is intimacy.

Communication As an Act of Love

There are two convictions that are essential prerequisites for loving communication. The first is that we must think of ourselves as gifts to be given. The second is that we must regard others as gifts (sometimes tentatively and hesitantly) offered to us. The exchange of these gifts is *communication*. It is clearly an act of gracious hospitality to welcome another into our confidence. Likewise, it is gracious of others to take us into the places where they live and work, and into their secret rooms. But this will happen only if communication is seen as an act of love. The only gift of any worth that I have to give you is myself. The only gift of value that you can offer me is the gift of yourself through self-disclosure. If we are not willing to run the risks involved in this exchange of gifts, we have really given each other nothing. We can have a relationship only of need, not of love. If our love for one another is to survive, communication is not really a luxury; it is a necessity.

If either of us falls into the deception of sharing self as a ploy, it will ruin everything. I must not want to communicate so that I will feel better, but only so that you may know me better. And I must not share myself with you so that you will react in the very way I had in mind. I don't share myself with you with the hope that you will feel responsible for me, or solve my problems, or feel guilty. I share myself with you only to let you know who I am and what it is really like to be me. I ask you to take my sharing in gentle and sensitive hands. But I do not have any hidden agendas. Do with it whatever you will. It is my gift to you.

We must not be deceived into thinking that communication makes one person out of two. You must always remain you, and I must always keep my own identity. You are you and I am I. We each think our own thoughts, retain our own preferences, make our own choices (and compromise only when necessary). This is the way it was in the beginning, is now, and ever shall be. In communicating with you, I don't want to look into a mirror and find your face there. Nor do I want you to march to my drums. The beauty of our communication will be a shared celebration of our differences. We are each unique. What it is like to be me is not what it is like to be you. However, if you will take me into your unique world and share it with me, I will certainly be enriched by this sharing. And if I welcome you into my private world, you will forever be richer for having known me.

Speaking in Communication

There are so many things I have to share with you. There is my *past*. It's not a simple statement of biographical facts. I must tell you about my laughter and my tears, about my successes and my failures. I must tell you about my *memories,* the ones that have shaped and directed my life. God gave us memories so that we could have roses in December. Some of mine are suffused with sunlight. Others were recorded in darkness and play only to a sad accompaniment. I must tell you about my unique *vision of reality,* the way I see things: myself, the other people in my life, the world about me, and the God I worship and pray to. I must share, too, my *hidden secrets,* my *hopes,* and my *values.*

But somehow, more important than all of these, I must tell you about my *feelings.* Some are light, others are dark; some are beautiful, others seem ugly to me. But they are all mine. I can't really explain them. I can only describe them to you. I do know that my roots are many and tangled. Some of my feelings are nourished at root level. They come from places and experiences stored so deep in me that I have never really explored them. But this much I know: my feelings are mine, and when I share them with you, I have a sense of sharing my most sensitive self with you. My feelings encapsulate my whole personal history, the experiences that have shaped my vision. My feelings depend, too, on my physical condition, my food intake and sleep supply. And though we use common labels, like anger and affection, no one has ever felt as I do. Somehow I know that when I share my feelings with you, I am sharing my one and only self.

One more thing. And I want to say this clearly. I want you to know this forever: *I assume full responsibility for these feelings.* I know that I must be, in my communication, an owner and not a blamer. Blaming is a game. It removes me from reality. Blaming is essentially a way of shifting responsibility and maintaining power over others. Blaming wants to nail its victims to the cross. Toxic adults want to lay all their personal miseries at the doorstep of their parents. Others didn't understand them or give them enough love. It is a futile game, which only serves as an excuse to rationalize the things I cannot accept about myself. Blaming is dumping my own feeling of guilt and shame on you. "I would have been all right, if only . . ." It really doesn't matter in human relationships who is "right" and who is "wrong." In blaming, everybody loses. The so-called winner can feel good or smug for a while, but the loser lies in wait for the chance to get even. The blamer loses contact with reality. The blamee feels like a garbage dump. The blaming game is only one of the games people play, as a counterfeit or substitute for relating. How true it is that "growth begins where blaming ends."

Owners versus blamers. It is quite easy to tell the difference. Owners always make "I" statements, while blamers tend to make "You" statements. "I felt angry" is an "I" statement. It is the statement of an owner who knows that anger has arisen out of something in him or herself. "You made me angry!" is the accusation statement of a blamer. It scapegoats the listener, shifts the responsibility for anger from the speaker onto the listener. Owners get to know themselves, and they mature. Blamers live in a make-believe but bitter world. Separated from reality by their blaming, they never really do get to know themselves or others. Unfortunately, they never grow up.

In trying to share myself with you, I will be tempted to cover up my vulnerable places. I will want to close off certain rooms because they contain secret weaknesses. I can so easily show you my trophy room of successes, but I don't want you to see the scars of my failures. If I do conceal my vulnerability, my weaknesses, my failures, I have not really shared my complete self with you. I have edited my sharing, shown you only the parts I wanted you to see. You will sense this, I am sure, and you will want to do the same thing. You will want to edit your sharing. But if I do put my whole self, warts and all, on the line, you will sense that I have taken a chance and have trusted you. Everything human is contagious. You will want to do the same. Like love, communication is a decision and a commitment.

Lastly, as a speaker, I must be careful not to judge you. I must try to educate myself to the mystery of each unique human being. Each three-pound, three-ounce human brain is more complicated than the most sophisticated computer. The millions of experiences stored in our brains are all somehow activated in everything we do and say. I know that you make psychological sense even when you are not making logical sense. I know that if I had your genes and family, if I had grown up in your neighborhood and had attended the schools you went to, I might be more like you than like what I am right now. So my admission here and now and forevermore is that I do not have X-ray eyes. If I seem to see through you, it is only my pretense and perhaps a projection of myself. I will sincerely respect the mystery that is you and the mystery that is me.

Listening in Communication

True listening, empathic listening, is indeed a rarely developed talent. If you or I should encounter five good listeners in a lifetime, we would be doing very well. First of all, I should be listening because I really want to know what it is like to be you. This means I will hear much more than the words you use. I will hear the emotions that vibrate in your voice. I will see the facial expressions and notice the body language that accompany your words. I won't be mentally preparing my own response to your sharing. At the end I will probably just nod and thank you most sincerely. I will tell you how grateful I am for your gift. I will promise to treat your confidences with a gentle respect.

Even though God gave us two ears and only one mouth, most of us are not good listeners. Most of us listen only long enough to shoot from the lip—to offer a little advice, tell an anecdote from the past, narrate a few stories of our own experiences. Sometimes we cast ourselves in the role of problem solvers. Or we take over the conversation by offering a survey of our own lives. Sometimes we expose our own inability to listen by closing off the speaker. We yawn, get visibly distracted, ask an unrelated question, or simply change the subject. Some of us find silence painful, and so we leap in to fill the gaps.

A good listener has tried in the past to be a good speaker, too. So good listeners know how hard it is to open up. If I am a good listener, I will interrupt only to ask you for a clarification of your meaning or for a detail I find missing. My interruptions will never intentionally derail you. I will try to supply the atmosphere you need to give me your gift. Obviously, it takes work and practice to become a good listener. But most of all, it requires a real capacity for empathy, a patient curiosity that wants to know what it is really like to be you.

A phrase that is familiar to most of us is "listening with the head and the heart." To be purely logical and deal only with ideas is listening only with the head. It will prove very discouraging for most speakers. Someone has pleaded, "Please hear what I am not saying." Almost everyone has an instinctual understanding of this. There are times when we just can't find the right words or the courage to say those words. We have to hope that the heart of the listener will supply those meanings. It is almost a truism that the least important things in communication are the words themselves. Joy and sorrow, affection and discouragement, hope and despair are conveyed in so many ways other than words. These realities can be grasped only by the heart. And they will be grasped only by the heart that is committed to love.

Semantics and Other Problems in Communication

Words are signs. Unfortunately, the reality symbolized by the same word-sign may be different for different people. One person may be happy to be called "sweet" while another may bristle at the very thought. It is a fact: words mean different things to different people. Everyone who has ever spoken to a group knows that each person in the audience is hearing a slightly different message. For example, "I am anxious about Monday" could mean one of several things. *Anxious* could mean "fearful." It could also mean "eager" or even "excited."

Both speaker and listener must be aware of this problem. The practice called shared meaning can offer some clarification. The speaker asks the listener to relate back what he or she has heard. Then both speaker and listener can arrive at some satisfaction that the message sent is the same as the message received.

Then there is the problem of prejudice. If I am right, we are all filled with prejudices of all sorts. For example, the names we like are probably those of people we have liked in the past. The names we don't like are probably those of people we didn't like. We are prejudiced with regard to almost everything, including food, colors, styles, races, and religions. A prejudice is a premature judgment. The judgment is premature because it is made on false or incomplete evidence. In the act of prejudice, the mind exercises the closure of a judgment before it has all the facts. Usually this happens because of emotional forces, conscious or unconscious.

It is obvious that prejudice can invade and undermine communication. If I carry a little checklist with me into every conversation, I will listen to see if you agree with me, to see how you check out. Instead of listening to learn what it is like to be you, I will be running down my list to see if you are one of "the good guys." Also, prejudice may close down my mind to all that is good in you because I recall something you said years ago. I gave you a "batting average" at that time, and I refuse to reconsider. Finally, there may be something I don't like about you. It could be your appearance, your mannerisms, or your political persuasion. If I let this one source of aversion keep me from opening to you or listening empathically to you, I have become the victim of prejudice.

Another obstacle to communication is imagination. If something is not said explicitly, imagination tends to fill in all the missing details. For example, you may have a vision problem. So when you look at another person, you tend to squint a bit. Your eyes narrow noticeably. If you do not tell me that you like me, I will probably imagine that you don't. I can tell by the way you look at me. When imagination supplies for communication, misunderstanding is inevitable. Now this possibility imposes a burden on both speaker and listener. The speaker should try to leave as few gaps as possible for the imagination of the listener. But, the listener must also check out his or her interpretations. "I read you as being quite upset with me. Is this true, or am I just imagining it?"

The Temptation to Quit

I'm sure that everyone has seen or heard the motto "Winners never quit. Quitters never win." Apart from the "rah, rah" hype, there is a truth here that is applicable to communication. There are times when the best lines of communication fall in the midst of some storm. A misunderstanding, an argument, a rash judgment can easily interrupt the flow of good communication. I'm sure that something like this happens at intervals to everyone.

The crisis is a test of one's determination. It is also a time to claim ownership instead of making accusations and blaming others. We blamers are always tempted to think that it is a question of good or bad, right or wrong. We want to figure out who has the problem and why. Excuse me for correcting myself in public, but none of the above categories applies here. If I give up on communication, I have to take full responsibility for this. I have to say that because of something in me, I have ceased trying to understand what it is like to be you. Oh, it is possible that one of us or even both of us may have an erroneous opinion or make a false judgment. But that is no reason to go off in a sulk or demand an apology. Love is not that small, and communication is an act of love or it is nothing. Part of the decision-commitment of love, I am sure, is the decision to keep trying and the commitment to persevere in communication.

A relationship is always stronger when two people survive a crisis. It is something like a broken bone. Nature throws out additional calcium around the break, so that the bone is actually stronger after the mending process is over. Most of us are at times tempted to quit, to give up, to blame, to go off looking for consolation and understanding from someone else. I think it is highly important to reerect the lines of communication, to keep trying. The relationship will forever be stronger and more durable because of these efforts and this commitment.

Processing These Ideas about Communication

1. *Locate Your Catastrophic Fears of Communication.* A catastrophic fear of an object or activity usually results from the anticipation of the worst thing that could happen. Try to get in touch with your own fears of good communication. What is the worst thing that could happen if you were an open and honest person with everyone? (Obviously, this does not mean to imply that we should tell all our secrets to everyone.) What is the worst thing that could happen if you were a truly empathic listener? What is the one specific thing about "intimacy" that frightens you most?

2. *Write a Page on "What It Is Like to Be Me."* Put your most profound self on paper. Then give that page to your closest partner in communication. Ask that person if what you have written really describes the person you project. Most of us have a private person and a public person. Are yours the same? Do you think people really know you? If not, is this because you have not opened yourself up, or because others have not really listened to you?

3. *Write a Second Page on "What It Is Like to Be You (Another)."* Try to describe your friend, confidant, or spouse at an in-depth level. Be sure you present your description as tentative, merely your impression. We can never infallibly tell others what they have said, but we can tell them what we have heard. You can share what you have observed and how you have interpreted. Do this, and then ask, "Have I been a good listener? Do I make you want to say, 'Thank God, someone finally knows what it is like to be me!'?"

Remember

"We are as sick as we are secret." And we are as healthy as we are able to give freely and to receive gratefully.

PRACTICE 9

We must learn to enjoy the good things of life.

The Talmud is a collection of rabbinical wisdom that dates back to the time of Jesus. One of the lines in the Talmud that has caught my attention is this: "Everyone will be called to account for all the legitimate pleasures which he or she has failed to enjoy." Most of us, I suspect, have never even thought about this. God's will is that we enjoy all the good things he has provided.

We are pilgrims. We are on our way to a holy and happy place: our Father's house. When I think of this, I think of the pilgrims who once landed on our eastern coast. We might imagine them setting out from that eastern coast determined to get to California. Supposing they kept their eyes down and their noses to the grindstone. Suppose they kept grumbling and mumbling, "We've got to get to California." Think of all the marvelous experiences and beauty they would miss. The skies and lakes, the sunrises and sunsets. The changing of the seasons: from the springtime through the summer and fall to the whiteness of winter. How

*foolish these pilgrims with downcast eyes and dreary
determination.*

*So many of us are like these foolish pilgrims. What-
ever we are determined to do and wherever we are
determined to go, we become so preoccupied that we
miss much of the beauty along the way. We lose the
art of enjoying. Somehow I am sure that the Talmud
is right: Enjoyment is an art God wants all of us to
cultivate.*

> *"A cheerful heart is a good medicine,
> but a downcast spirit dries up the bones."*
> Proverbs 17:22

Enjoyment Is Also an Inside Job

Just as happiness comes from a source inside each of us, so does
enjoyment. As the old Roman philosopher Epictetus tried to tell
his contemporaries, "It's all in the way you look at it." Remember
the two men who looked out of prison bars; one saw mud, the
other stars. Enjoyment is more a mind-set than a set of circumstances. Enjoyment is actually more a choice than a chance. We
all know that some people enjoy life much more than others do.
And I think we all know that those who enjoy life are not necessar-
ily more gifted or fortunate than the joyless. It's just that some
have their interior dials set to enjoy life, while others seem to
insist on struggling through life.

The intention to enjoy seems to be one of those attitudes or
mind-sets that is with us from childhood. It almost seems that
we came into this world asking, "What is life for?" Somehow the
answer got filled in, and we drew our own conclusions. Of course,
it is impossible to say where or from whom we got the answer

to our question. The important thing is that we did get an answer. What we heard may not have been what was said, but it did become our answer. It set our expectations, told us what to anticipate. The rest of our lives has been a self-fulfilling prophecy.

Eventually we learned to look at reality, at life itself, through the lenses of this developed mind-set. We came to expect life to be enjoyable or difficult. We woke up each day with this mind-set, and it colored all our days and all our experiences. Sometimes it is very hard for us to admit, but through this mind-set we ourselves have shaped and determined our own experiences. We have made our experiences, our days, and our lives happy or sad. Please understand that the basic attitude or mind-set was probably programmed into us very early in life. It was the result of suggestions from others and of our interpretation of these suggestions. In any case, this attitude or mind-set gradually became a part of us and has set the dials of our minds to struggle or to enjoy, or something in-between.

The Adult Children of Alcoholics and Early Programming

One of the more recent developments in the field of alcoholism recovery is a group called ACOA, the Adult Children of Alcoholics. Two college students whom I recognized as children of alcoholics helped me to understand what happens. Both were the children of alcoholic fathers. In both cases the fathers had stopped drinking while the students were in early adolescence. However, the messages from an actively alcoholic parent were already recorded on the so-called parent tapes of both. The students described these messages as follows: "Don't touch . . . don't talk . . . don't get close to anyone . . . don't allow yourself to feel . . . don't touch or allow yourself to be touched . . . always stay on the alert and be ready to adjust to the unpredictable."

Of course, each adult child of an alcoholic looks and reacts differently, but in general, life is colorless through these lenses. There seems to be an emotional numbness, a fear of relating to others, a distrust of one's own reactions. Sometimes it looks as though the whole world is having a large and happy picnic. The adult child of an alcoholic doesn't feel invited. He or she stands alone, looking sadly through the fence.

The adult child of an alcoholic, like all of us, must readjust and revise. It can be done, but old habits will have to be unlearned and new habits will have to be practiced. Experiment with the next hour of your life. Decide that you are going to enjoy it. Determine that you will appreciate the good things of that hour, that you will take advantage of the opportunities offered in that next hour. Every time you do this, you will be cultivating the habit of enjoyment. Eventually this habit will become a permanent mind-set.

Once I taught a young woman who seemed to be very gifted. She was intellectually bright, physically beautiful, athletically talented. However, the expression on her face was always strained and pained. When she came in to talk to me, I mentioned that her face belied her goodness and giftedness. She explained to me that she knew all about it. "You see," she said, "I am adopted. My adoptive parents never told me this, but I always thought that if I ever displeased them, I would have to go back to the orphanage. I was always walking on eggshells. I felt sure of no one's love."

So she was spending her life continuing to walk on eggshells. She was trying not to displease people. She was afraid that they would send her back to the orphanage. It was again a case of an inherited vision in need of revision. But fortunately that revision is now in process, and the person in question is gradually being transformed into a happy person capable of enjoyment.

In ACOA meetings, letting someone else deprive you of happiness is called "stinkin' thinkin'." We worry about all the wrong things, we sweat the small stuff, and we become preoccupied with deadlines and worried about decisions. We allow other things and persons to deprive us of the enjoyment of life that is God's will.

A Girl Named Betty
and a Man Named Frank

A former student of mine, a quiet and reserved girl, came back to see me. We chatted for a few moments, and then I asked her if she was using her R.N. (nursing) degree. "No," she replied. "You see, I am dying. I have terminal leukemia." Of course, I gasped. When I recovered from the shock, I asked Betty what it was like. "What is it like to be twenty-four, when you think that your whole life lies ahead of you, and then suddenly you are counting the days left?" In her usual reserved and peaceful way, she replied, "I'm not sure that I can explain this, but these are the happiest days of my life. When you think that there are years ahead, it is so easy to put things off. You say to yourself, 'I'll stop and smell the flowers next spring.' But when you know that the days of your life are limited, you stop to smell the flowers and to feel the warm sunlight *today.* Because of the disease I am suffering from, I have had several spinal taps. It is a painful procedure. However, my boyfriend held my hand during these spinal taps. I think I was more aware of the comfort of his hand in mine than of the needle being inserted into my spine."

We talked for a long time about dying and the perspectives it affords for full living. I had always heard that no one can live fully unless that person knows that life will someday come to an end. Betty helped me to understand why that is true. She is dead now. Leukemia eventually claimed her life. But she left me with a deeper understanding of the need to enjoy all the good things of this life. It was as if God was saying to me through her, "You are a pilgrim making a journey, but do try to enjoy the trip."

Another person who has helped me to understand the mind-set of enjoyment was a man named Frank. Everyone liked Frank. He was warm and kind. He was always smiling. Frank liked "little people" as much as he appreciated "little things." Then Frank suddenly died. Although he had at one time been rather wealthy, Frank did not leave much of an estate in property or investments. But much like Betty, Frank had left me a last legacy. It was two pages of "A List of My Special Pleasures." Good old Frank had actively cultivated his capacity to enjoy by listing his daily joys. He worked all his adult life at the "mind-set" of enjoyment. He had set the dials of his mind to enjoy all the humor, the rainbows and butterflies of life. According to his list, Frank enjoyed many things during his days on this earth, including scenic trails, sunrises, writing congratulatory notes, birds in flight, picture albums, the Boston Pops orchestra, playing Scrabble in front of a fireplace. The last four entries on his long list were all the same: "ice cream, ice cream, ice cream, ice cream." I'm sure that Frank had his private sufferings, but somehow he always managed to enjoy the good things of life. In this he will always be an important role model for me.

A Roll Call of Demons

I am sure that the mind-set of enjoyment cannot be an overlay type of mind-set. It cannot be used as a simple coverup for gloom and struggle. That would be putting one mask over another. We must first get in touch with the reasons we hold back from enjoyment. Psychologists have a picnic with this subject. There are so many possible reasons that can diminish our capacity for enjoyment. Each of us must explore our own inner spaces to exorcise our own personal demons. In *The Screwtape Letters,* C. S. Lewis describes the instructions of the chief devil to his henchmen. "Tempt this person in this way, but with this other person, don't use that technique. It would be wasted. Try this approach," and so forth. I'm sure that each of us is tempted by a unique and tailor-made obstacle to enjoyment.

With some of us, it may be a direct message from our childhood. It may be that no one ever told us, but we concluded from what we saw and experienced, that life is not to be enjoyed. Morbid messages heard and recorded by us during our early years tend to keep playing in us for life, unless we identify and disown them. We might have heard things like: "Life is a struggle. Don't expect a break from anyone. Wait till you get out in the cold, cruel world. You'll see."

Many of us are self-punishing. We remember chapter and verse of all our mistakes. We keep a librarian's record of our sins. One great psychiatrist says that there may be a God in heaven who forgives us our sins, but we are much more reluctant to forgive ourselves. It is as though we have judged ourselves and recorded our failures in every muscle, fiber, and brain cell of our being. A guilt complex is certainly one of the enjoyment inhibitors with which many of us human beings have to contend.

Elsewhere we have discussed the terrible toll of perfectionism. We called it "a suicide course" because it certainly deprives us of the fullness of life. Because we are not perfect, and because nothing we do is ever perfect, we leave ourselves only room for failure. And when failure becomes the color of our days and nights, discouragement and depression soon close in on us.

Every one of us has an inferiority complex. Those who do not seem to have one are only pretending. Their pretense may even become self-deceptive, but it is a deception. We all have areas of insecurity. Inferiority is a relative term. It is the opposite or counterpart of superiority. Inferiority always implies comparison. I compare myself with others. I find that others are smarter, better looking, more capable, or more virtuous than I am. Comparison is always the beginning of inferiority feelings. And it is almost impossible to enjoy anything else when we do not enjoy ourselves.

All-or-nothing thinking can also undermine enjoyment. For example, I could reason that because I am not all that I should be, I must be nothing. Or because I am not completely honest, I must be a total phony. It takes a little quiet time and some reflection to be comfortable as a fraction, but that is what we all are. Part of us is good and beautiful, but there is another part that remains unconverted. Part of us is light and part of us is dark. Part believes, another part doubts. Part is loving, part is selfish. Now, what we have called all-or-nothing thinking does not tolerate fractions very well. It does not like the gray area between black and white. And this all-or-nothing thinking doesn't even know the word *process,* let alone the reality. It obviously doesn't relish gradual growth and change because it wants to be all one cut of cloth, without shades and nuances of color. It has an enormous capacity to diminish and deny happiness. Everything has to go completely well, everyone has to be won over and convinced, and every grade has to be an *A* or it's the dark night of the soul.

Finally, we should check out our assumptions. Some of us have built our lives on irrational assumptions. For example, "I can't enjoy myself when I am alone." These irrational assumptions of ours have a way of turning into self-fulfilling prophecies. The person who assumes that there is no happiness in solitude will never be happy when alone. The person who assumes that other persons and things make us happy will always be disappointed in the end. Perhaps the most fatal assumption is to believe that "I am this way and that is that!" I remember having long discussions with a man who felt that since his early life was unhappy, he was doomed and destined to a life of unhappiness. Whenever I suggested that he could change, he protested that I was not listening. It was very difficult to shake his assumption.

Driving Out the Demons

Behavior modification theorists assure us that we can change without understanding exactly how we got into our "denial-of-enjoyment" condition. The only important thing is to change, and this can be done by contriving a system of rewards and punishments. For example, let us suppose that your personal demon, whatever it is, rears its ugly head. If you win and enjoy something despite your demon, reward yourself. If your demon wins, inflict some minor chastisement upon yourself. For example, wear a rubber band around your wrist, and every time you cave in to your demon, snap the rubber band.

Obviously (to me), it will help us to understand the nature of our problem. If I have an otherwise very pleasant evening, but allow one small incident to ruin everything, I should really try to get in touch with why I do this. If I enjoy a pleasant dinner, see a wonderful show, and return home unhappy because it cost me six dollars to park the car, I should ask some questions of myself. Let us suppose that only one person in a large group doesn't seem to like me, although everyone else does. Let us further suppose that I get upset by this one person. This would seem to be matter for personal investigation. Someone has said that if you name your demon, you tame it. It would be most helpful, I would think, to name and expose the little demon in charge of denying delight to me. As one psychiatrist put it: "We all know we could be happy, but there is always a big *if* or a big *but*. Well, I say it's time for us to get off our *buts*." What are the "ifs" and "buts" that limit my enjoyment of life? Sometimes, if the insight comes clearly and powerfully enough, it can bring with it a life-transforming effect.

Once I produced a long listing of the masks people wear. I gave the wearers nicknames, like Elmer Egghead, Peppermint Patty the People Pleaser, Dennis Doormat, Polly Porcupine. My hope was that each of us could find the mask we were wearing and proceed to take it off. Many friends of mine reported, "But I see a little of myself in all of your descriptions." When I thought about it, I had to agree. I also saw a little of myself in each of the proposed masks. I think I played each of the roles depending on the circumstances, and so forth. But there was one—Harry the Helper—that kept haunting me. I realized that I was assuming this role more often than the rest. I would never be totally honest about myself because then others would want to help me, and that would confuse everything. Without words I insisted that "I am the helper and you are the helpee. Please get that straight, and please stay in your assigned role."

When I go over the delight-denying demons, I see that all of them bother me at some time or another. But there is one, perfectionism, that seems to be my major problem. It then becomes a matter of divide and conquer. I have isolated my tendency to be a helper-rescuer-enabler and my penchant for perfectionism. Now I am working on them. I know that it is a question of gradual change, unlearning old and practiced habits and replacing them with new and life-giving habits. So, I am trying to be patient, but this is hard for us perfectionists. However, I have to be honest and say that every little victory seems to brighten the sky of my world and to widen my capacity for enjoyment and the fullness of life. And with the passage of time, I seem to enjoy the journey more and more.

Processing These Ideas about Enjoying the Good Things of Life

1. *Name Your Demon.* Which of the devils discussed seems to haunt your personal premises most often and undermine your capacity for enjoyment?

a. Parent Tapes (the messages that keep playing inside you): Specifically, what are these messages?

b. A Guilt Complex: Do you think you are self-punishing? Do you hate yourself for your mistakes? Do you rehash your regrets?

c. Perfectionism: Do you attach your value to your production? Do you believe that you ought to be perfect? Is it important for you to impress and please others? Do you get discouraged by failure?

d. Inferiority Complex: Do you feel inferior to many others to whom you compare yourself? How do you measure your worth? Do you believe that you are who you are supposed to be, and fully equipped to do what you are supposed to do?

e. All-or-Nothing Thinking: Do you really believe in slow growth and process? Are there gray areas for you between black and white? If you tell the truth 100 times and lie once, what would you call yourself: a truth teller or a liar?

f. Irrational Assumptions: Are there any enjoyment-denying assumptions from which you proceed? Do you really believe that we are all supposed to be happy?

2. *Make a List of Your "Favorite Things."* Of course, this will be an ongoing procedure. Keep expanding your list. Sometimes it helps to go back over this list, after it has been composed, and ask, "Do I fail to enjoy these 'favorite things' at times?" At the end of every day, list the things you really enjoyed during that day. Does a pattern emerge and maybe tell you something about yourself? (I found "helping others" occurred on my enjoyment list most often. You will recall that I'm good old Harry the Helper.)

Remember

You will someday be called to account for all the legitimate pleasures you failed to enjoy. So, go ahead, Pilgrim, enjoy the journey!

We must make prayer a part of our daily lives.

The Jesuit novitiate was spartan in those good old days. We talked in Latin, greeting each other with the Latin term Carissime, which is translated, "Dearly Beloved." Oh, my! The master of novices told us we had been called out of the world and, of course, we believed him. In fact, one of the novices told a bus driver he was surprised at the raise in fare. Then the novice added, "When I was in the world, it was only fifty cents." That raised the eyebrows and curiosity of the bus driver. The poor man did a double take, then quizzically asked the novice, "Excuse me, fella, but where do you think you are?"

For me the most puzzling part of the novitiate experience was prayer. It was a wilderness. When the master of novices asked me if I had trouble with sleep during the morning meditation, I promptly assured him, "Oh, no, I go right off every morning." The most tantalizing part of it all was watching the "quakers and shakers" (as I secretly called them) in the chapel. I wanted to ask them, "Do you know something I

*don't? You're getting through, aren't you?" But this
kind of questioning and sharing was not allowed, so
I just kept wondering.*

*I identified with the poor moth who tried to get
through the screen to the light on my desk. Poor guy
kept hitting his head on the screen and trying again.
He never made it.*

*Then came "Mayday." I was sure it was all a hoax.
I was quite sure I didn't believe in any of it. But the
master of novices told me to be patient, although I
wasn't sure what it was that I was being patient for.
I guess I forgot to ask what I could expect.*

*Then one night in the early spring, God touched
me. I felt filled with his undeniable presence. I remember thinking, "If this is what happiness is, I have never
been happy before. This is a taste of new wine." I
remember standing there crying tears of relief. There
really was a God. And he had been inside me all the
time.*

The Critical Question

Perhaps the one question that most divides believers among themselves is this: Does God really interact with us? It is said that
Thomas Jefferson, who considered himself a religious man, denied
this willingness of God to interact with us. In fact, he is said to
have razored out of his personal Bible all the passages that describe God entering human history and dialoguing with human
beings. There are even some theologians who deny this willingness of God to become involved with us. And many of us who in
theory may not want to accept a noninvolved God, in fact seem
to think of God this way. There are many of us who really expect
God to be silent and distant. Occasionally we throw our prayers
and gifts over the high wall that separates us from God. We hope
that he hears, but we do not expect an answer.

The question is critical because all relationships thrive on communication. Even on the purely human level, without an active communication there can be no relationship. I think that the same thing is true of our relationship with God. Only the communication in this relationship with God has a special name: prayer.

The Barrier to Communication: The Masks We Wear

But communication is rarely easy. Unfortunately, most of us put on our masks, dress up in the costumes of our chosen roles, and begin reciting our well-rehearsed lines. The problem is that the masks, the costumes, and the lines are not really us. They are usually only our adaptations to reality. They are also barriers to real sharing and honest dialogue. You know this and I know this, in theory at least. If I put on an act, no matter what the act is, you cannot possibly interact with me. I have not given you a real person with whom to interact. So we try to meet somewhere on a stage, and we recite memorized lines to each other. I would like to submit as my opinion that God can truly interact with us only to the extent that we are real. And this, my sisters and brothers, is not easy. Being real, totally open and totally honest, usually takes a long time.

Of course, there are many types of prayers, just as there are many ways of communicating. But in essence, there is always in prayer some form of dialogue. It may not be a dialogue of words, though words usually find their way into the exchange. We humans often say more to each other by a smile or an embrace than we are able to say by words. But gestures and facial expressions can often be misinterpreted unless they are accompanied by words of explanation. Whatever the type of prayer one feels inclined to, the essence of communication is, as always, an honest sharing of self.

The Sincere Desire to Pray

Admittedly, there are times when we can engage in wordless prayer. But there is one thing without which we simply cannot pray. That is the *sincere desire to pray*. At first none of us wants to admit it, but we are all afraid of getting too close to God. A thousand questions and doubts flood into us at the very thought of being close to God. What will God say to me? What will God ask of me? Where will God lead me? The unknown is always a little frightening. And in this case, the stakes are high. My whole life is involved. God might shatter my whole construct, rearrange all my values.

Furthermore, I enter into every other dialogue as an equal. My thoughts are just as good as yours. My choices are mine, and you have no right to interfere. I did not come into this world to live up to your expectations, and you did not come into the world to live up to mine. It is quite different in the dialogue with God, who says, "Be still and know that I am God." As Albert Einstein once said, "When I approach this God, I must take off my shoes and tread lightly, for I am on sacred ground."

The High Price of Prayer: Surrender

Another essential condition for successful prayer is *surrender*. The very word usually terrifies us. But the fact of the matter is that the posture of surrender is a nonnegotiable condition for prayer. I remember reading a story written by a woman I have never met. In her article she described her humble origins—a cold-water flat, saving pennies for a "treat." Then she met her husband-to-be. He was the personification of her dreamed-about hero. She could not believe her ears when he asked her to marry him. Among other things, he had some wealth, so they moved to a suburb, where there was warm water, large windows, and green lawns. There were flowers in the summertime. And soon there was the marvel of children. It was all Jean had ever wanted.

Then she began feeling physically sick. Eventually she went to a doctor, and he put her in the hospital for tests. She was not at all prepared for it when her doctor looked at her sadly and said, "Your liver has stopped working." She almost screamed at him: "Are you telling me that I am dying?" With downcast eyes, he said solemnly, "We have done all we can." Then he turned and silently left her hospital room.

She felt a fire of anger ignite inside her. In her fury she wanted to tell God off. So, in her hospital gown and robe, she struggled through the corridors on her way to the chapel. It was to be a face-to-face confrontation. She felt so weak, she had to support herself by bracing against the wall as she moved along. When she entered the chapel, it was dark. No one else was there. So she proceeded up the center aisle on her way to the altar. Through what seemed like an endless journey from her room to the chapel, she had been preparing her speech: "Oh God, you are a fraud, a real phony. You have been passing yourself off as love for two thousand years. But every time anyone finds a little happiness, you pull out the rug from under her feet. Well, I just want you to know that I have had it. I see through you."

In the center aisle and near the front of the chapel, she fell. She was so weak, she could hardly see. Her eyes could barely read the words woven into the carpet at the step into the sanctuary. She read and then repeated the words: "LORD, BE MERCIFUL TO ME, A SINNER." Suddenly, all the angry words, all the desire to tell God off was gone. All that was left was: "Lord, be merciful to me, a sinner." Then she put her tired head down over her crossed arms, and listened. Deep within herself she heard: "All of this is a simple invitation to ask you to turn your life over to me. You have never done that, you know. The doctors here do their best to treat you, but I alone can cure you."

In the silence and darkness of that night, she turned her life over to God. She signed her blank check and turned it over to him to fill in all the amounts. It was the hour of God. It was the moment of her surrender.

Finding her way back to her room in the hospital, she slipped off into a deep sleep. The next day, after blood and urinalysis tests, the doctor gave her the hopeful news: "Your liver seems to be functioning again." Like Job in the Old Testament, God had led her to the brink, but only to invite her surrender. It is an important prerequisite for the communication of prayer. "Thy will be done!" is an enormous and frightening concession. It leaves us standing naked and defenseless. No more masks, no protective barriers. Just this: "Be still and know that I am God."

The Possibility of Prayer and Our Concept of God

We all have a different idea of God. Maybe intellectually some of us might define God using the same words. But we are more than just intellects. Of course, no one can say for sure where his or her idea of God has come from. But it is there, and it causes definite emotional reactions in us. Our concept of God propels us forward or it holds us back. Where did we get our idea of God? Our parent tapes and early religious instructions, our experiences, our imaginations, and even our programmed reactions to authority figures helped forge our concept of God. The Book of Genesis tells us that we are made in God's image and likeness, but it is inevitable that we also shape our concept of God in our own human image and likeness. We make God "one of us." We project impatience into God. We imagine God turning away from us. We think a thousand things that could never be. The fact is this: God is love, according to the Scriptures. God's nature is to love. Of course, divine love is far greater than we could possibly imagine, but this we can know: whatever God does is done out of love.

The Experience of God and Alcoholics Anonymous

One large group of believers in this God of love are the people in the Alcoholics Anonymous Fellowship. One of the founders of the movement and coauthor of the famous Twelve Steps program was a man named William G. "Bill" Wilson. Within the last twenty-five years, his correspondence with psychiatrist Carl Jung has been published. At the time the correspondence began, in January 1961, Bill Wilson wrote gratefully to Jung about Jung's role in the foundation of Alcoholics Anonymous. It seems that Jung had treated one Roland H. (The members of Alcoholics Anonymous protect anonymity by so designating themselves.)

After repeated treatments, Jung told Roland H. that he was hopelessly alcoholic. Wilson insists that Jung's acknowledgment of Roland's hopelessness became the first foundation stone of Alcoholics Anonymous. The first of the famous Twelve Steps is to admit personal powerlessness, the unmanageability of one's life. After this, when Roland asked Jung if there was any other hope, Jung told him that there might be, provided Roland could become the subject of a spiritual or religious experience, in short, a genuine conversion. Wilson thanks Jung effusively for pointing out how such an experience can provide the needed motivation when nothing else can. It was this suggestion that resulted in the second and third steps: belief in a loving and helpful God, and the turning over of one's life to this God.

It seems that Wilson himself was hopelessly addicted to alcohol at the same time that Roland H. was. Wilson's own doctor, a Dr. Silkworth, had also given him up for lost. Wilson admits, in his correspondence with Jung, that he cried out to God, begged for his help. In the same letter he acknowledges that there immediately came to him an "illumination of enormous impact and dimension." Bill Wilson felt that he could never adequately describe this moment. He knew only that his release from the alcohol obsession was immediate. "At once, I knew that I was a free man."

Wilson acknowledged to Jung that he had also gained a great insight from William James's *Varieties of Religious Experience*. He wrote to the psychiatrist that this book had given him the realization that most conversion experiences, whatever their variety, do have a common denominator at their depth, namely, "ego collapse." This ego collapse is a giving up on oneself and one's own powers.

In the wake of his own spiritual experience there came to Bill Wilson a vision of a society of alcoholics. He reasoned that if each sufferer were to carry the news of the scientific hopelessness of alcoholism to each new prospect, such a sharing would lay every newcomer wide open to a transforming spiritual experience. It was this concept that proved to be the foundation of such success as Alcoholics Anonymous has achieved over the years.

It is not surprising, then, that Alcoholics Anonymous is very openly a spiritual program. Of the well-known Twelve Steps, only the first step mentions alcohol. All the others, directly or indirectly, mention God. But of special interest to us here and now are the first three steps. *The first step* is to face the unmanageability of my life. Even though I am not personally an alcoholic or a member of Alcoholics Anonymous, I have learned so much from the wisdom of this movement. I have come to recognize and acknowledge that there are so many areas of my own life that are riddled with irrationality. My perfectionism, my hypersensitivity, my immaturity when things don't go my way, my desire to pout and punish others—all confront me with the fact that these are unmanageable areas of my life. My life has indeed become unmanageable. I have tried to change, but know now that I cannot succeed without help. *The second step* is to come to believe in a God who loves me and wants to help me. I have to believe that this gentle and caring God will help me if I will only let him. (This step is really hard for us Harry Helpers.) Such openness to God's help involves *the third step,* which is to turn my life over to God. As many AAs put it: "Let go and let God."

No one has to convince the members of Alcoholics Anonymous that prayer is necessary. These are people who have had to take off all the masks of sham and pretense. These are people who have come to believe in a gentle and loving God, a "Higher Power" who mends what is broken, who straightens what has been twisted and distorted, who enlightens what is dark, and who revives what has died in us. These are the people who have turned their lives over to this God. Such a concept of and surrender to God is an important prelude to prayer.

Making Peace
with My Weakness

Most of us have an instinctive fear of God that is based on our own weakness. We even fear other humans who we think can see right through us. We are indeed mistake makers, and sometimes our mistakes have been costly, to ourselves and to others. We either have to become comfortable with this human condition or go on pretending that it is not true. We have to go on hiding behind our pretending. Naturally, I am not suggesting that we simply cave in and give in to human weakness. I am suggesting that we must learn to be comfortable as fractions. We have all sinned and we will all sin again. For myself, it is extremely important to know the Jesus who comes as the Divine Physician, making highly personalized house calls on those of us who are sick. It is important for me to know the Jesus who is the Good Shepherd. I have to keep remembering that he is looking for us lost sheep and rejoicing when he finds us.

Again and again I have gone over the parable of the prodigal son. I am the prodigal son who has squandered my gifts on so many vanities and immaturities. I feel a deep remorse. I have been so ungrateful. I prepare my words carefully and fearfully: "Oh, I can't ask to be taken back as a son. Take me back as a hired hand. Please, just take me back." Armed with my act of contrition born of loneliness and need, I start homeward. My steps are tentative and uncertain. But my Abba-Father sees me coming and rushes down the road. He takes me into his arms and sobs in relief, "You're home. You know, that's all I've ever wanted. You're home." In his parable Jesus assures me that I am welcomed in this way by my loving Abba-God. I have had to read that parable again and again. I have had to make the long journey home more than once. Gradually I am coming to know the gentle love and the gracious mercy of God.

The World of the Spirit

A friend of mine recently told me the story of two fish swimming in the ocean. The little fish swims up to the big one and asks, "Excuse me. Where is the ocean?" The big fish answers, "You are in it." The little fish does not understand and tries to ask his question again: "I mean, can you tell me how to get into the ocean?" Again the big fish answers, "You are already in the ocean." The little fish swims away looking for someone else to answer his question.

My friend compares the question of the little fish to the question of those who ask, "What is spirituality? Where is the world of the spirit?" He pretends he is the bigger fish and says, "You're in it." Viktor Frankl, the Viennese psychiatrist, says that modern psychology has spent the last fifty years concentrating on the mind and the body. He complains that psychology has consistently neglected the human spirit and the world of the spiritual.

But we really have no choice. We are mind and body and spirit. We are "in it." We know when bodies are sick, and we bring them to our physicians. We know when minds are sick, and we entrust them to our psychiatrists. But spirits can get sick, too. Spirits can get starved, just as bodies can. They, too, need consistent nourishment and regular exercise. What are the symptoms when spirits get sick? We nourish grudges, we resent a lot of people, we find little meaning in life or human activity. We have a hard time enjoying. We are weak when strength is needed, and we become complainers and blamers. We are noticeably devoid of what the Scriptures call the "gifts of the Holy Spirit": love or charity, happiness, peace, patience, friendliness, kindness, loyalty, gentleness, and self-control.

When God made us, someone has suggested, we were made like Swiss cheese. We have a lot of holes in us that only God can fill. If we do not ask God to fill our emptiness, we will foolishly try to fill it ourselves. We brag, we lie, we gossip, collect trophies, drop names, show off, compete for the limelight, try to gain power over others, gulp at the fountains of sensual pleasure, and look for kicks. But in the end, we are left with the painful emptiness that only God can fill.

The college years are usually years of risk and revision. So it did not surprise me when one of my former students returned to tell me of an experiment he had made. At the end of his college days, he was still not sure if he believed or was merely brain-washed. So on his own he decided to spend a week as though there were no God. He would refrain from prayer, from going to church, from doing everything that faith enjoins. Then in the following week, he would live a life of intense faith, including much prayer and everything that is part of the faith-filled life. When he finished telling me of his experiment, he smiled and added, "What a difference! If I were ever to deny the importance of faith and prayer, I would have to deny my own experience. I could never do that."

The Hour of God

Usually the term *hour* has a neutral significance. It is purely an indication of time. However, in the Scriptures, the "hour of God" has a special religious significance. The hour of God indicates a turning point in a life, or in human history, through God's special intervention. The Lord asks us to be vigilant and ready because we cannot know in advance the "hour of God," the hour of God's coming to us with a special intervention. I am now old enough and wise enough to know that I cannot demand or produce this hour of God. God will come to me and to you in his way and at his hour. Sometimes we are tempted to stand like animal trainers, with our hoops. We urge God to come, to jump through our hoops, and now! But in the end we discover, sadly sometimes, that God is not a trained animal. God chooses his moments. God uses his means. Ours is only to be ready for these special moments. Sometimes God's hour seems to come at the very limit of our endurance. However, part of our trust in God is that God will come to us, in the best possible time and in the best possible way. I have to let you be you, and you have to let me be me. And we have to let God be God.

One of the values of what are called faith stories is that we can share God's "hours" in our lives. Of course, we cannot be naive. We cannot put full trust in everyone who is willing to tell us a story of personal experience. There is the "time test," which looks to see if the experience has had lasting effects. There is also the "reality test," which considers whether the experience has strengthened or weakened the storyteller's contact with reality. And finally, there is the "love" or "charity test," which studies whether or not the experience has deepened an individual's decision and commitment to love.

Some years ago, I wrote about my own hours of God. The little book was called *He Touched Me: My Pilgrimage of Prayer.* It was written in response to a request from a minister friend of mine. In the book, I admitted my many weaknesses and personal brokenness. Of course, I also talked of God's goodness to me. But when the manuscript was finished, I realized that the "whole world" would now know what a phony I had been. So I added in the text:

> I am not sure what my story has been worth to you. It may well be that you are far advanced in the dialogue of prayer and well beyond me. Some of the admissions I have made in these pages, especially those concerning my own weakness and infidelity, came hard for me. The thought of making them public in print causes a little tightening inside me. But I want to do it for you. The real gift of love is self-disclosure. Until we have given that, we have given nothing. And I hope that you will accept this gift as I have intended it: as an act of love.

This small book of 100 pages has resulted in many others sharing their faith story with me. In fact, I received about four or five letters a week for nearly two years. Hundreds of others had been touched by the same loving God and wanted to share their experience with me. One of the letters was from a young woman in the southeastern part of the United States. She admitted, without details, that she had led an evil life for many years. She said that suicide seemed to be the only way out of the moral mire in which she seemed to be stuck. Almost strangely, she wanted to die by drowning. She admitted that she had always fantasized the ocean as a big, soft, and watery mother, who "would rock me forever in the arms of its waves."

On the day she sought to execute her plans, she found the ocean a snarling beast rather than a soft and loving mother. It was a gray day, and the ocean was angry. But she said to herself, "Whether I am rocked in the arms of the waves or devoured by this snarling beast, I know that I must die. I must give myself to these waters." So she walked quietly along the deserted beach, as though she was saying good-bye to this world. Then she wrote that she heard a clear and distinct voice which told her to "stop, turn around, and look down." When she did this, all she could see were her own footprints in the sand. Then she watched as the ocean waves rushed in and obliterated her footprints. Then again the voice: "Just as you see the waves of the ocean washing away your footprints on the sand, so has my love and mercy erased all your past. I am calling you to live and to love, not to die." By instinct she knew it was the voice of God.

My correspondent told me that she turned away from the ocean, and soon discovered a new strength in the God who had spoken to her on that gray and deserted beach. She eventually found a happy and meaningful life. Then she added that "many years have passed since that eventful day, but I have never told anyone. I guess, for one thing, it is too personal. But there is another reason. My life is built on that moment, and I didn't want to hear anyone ridiculing it or me for my supposed naiveté. I didn't want anyone to laugh and say, 'Oh, you just didn't really want to die, so you made up a voice.' No, I have never told this to anyone else. But I do want to tell you. I want you to know of the hour of God in my life. It is my act of love for you. Take it in gentle hands."

I wrote a letter of gratitude. We have never corresponded since that time. But I still hold that treasure in "gentle hands." I am sure that the willingness of that good person to share God's goodness to her has rekindled in me a spirit of openness. She has strengthened my desire for God's intimacy. I will always be grateful to her.

A Suggested Form of Prayer

We have already said that there are many forms of prayer. I recently saw one I had never thought of. It starts out by looking at a "secular" picture and letting it stir prayerful thoughts and desires in the viewer. I like this approach because it seems to integrate faith into life. I look at the picture of a flower or a house, and I remember the special symbolism of love by flowers. Or, looking at the house, I recall that we will all be gathered someday into God's house. My mind and heart move forward from there into further prayerful images and thoughts.

What I would like to suggest is something similar. Begin by trying to tell God who you are at this time. I am told that whenever we think, we also verbalize our thoughts at least mentally. So verbalize to God who you are. Force yourself to paint this verbal portrait. At first it will be difficult. But going into deeper and deeper layers of self is a very helpful exercise in self-knowledge in addition to making for good prayer. And since everything is really God's gift, it helps to begin with a prayer for the gift of praying well. "Help me, loving God, to get to know myself and to know you. Help me to understand our relationship. Enlighten and empower me. Thank you." Then proceed with reflective questions like: Who am I? How do I feel today? What are the thoughts and feelings that have been rumbling around inside me during the last twenty-four hours? What has been most important to me? What person has meant most to me? What did I enjoy? What has caused me pain? Are there any special persons who played an important role in my recent life? What motives moved me into action? What did I really want to achieve, win, avoid? Overall, what am I doing with my life? Do I really want this?

I find that as I force myself to verbalize my answers to questions like these, I am actually getting to know myself better. Every day the answers are slightly different, as I peel off more layers and look into new corners of myself. Also, my moods change. Some days I feel tired of it all. Other days I am ready to move mountains. I also leave the "conversational door" open to God. We humans actually have many doors through which God can come into the dialogue. We have our *minds* into which God can put new ideas, insights, perspectives. We have our *wills* or *hearts* in which God can implant desires and put his strength. We have *emotions* so God can comfort us in our affliction or afflict us in our comfort. God can come into our emotions with peace or with challenge. We also have *imaginations,* which means that in our dialoguing, God can say words or even suggest pictures to us. When Robert asks Joan of Arc in Shaw's *Saint Joan,* "Do you really hear God's voice or is it the voice of your imagination?" Joan replies, "Both. That is the way God speaks to us, through our imaginations." We also have *memories,* and God can stir our memories in the prayer of reminiscence. God can also heal our hurting memories or transform them into helpful memories. All in all, there are these five ports of entry for God to come into our reflective prayer. The important thing is to know that our limits are God's opportunities.

At the end of prayer, I ask God for my needs. "Enlighten me to see and empower me to do the loving thing with this day in my life. Fill my dry wells with your love so that I can pass it on." I then mention the names of people I have promised to pray for. I ask God to bless them. I pray for the people I have hurt—some knowingly, others unknowingly. But I was too distracted with myself even to notice. I thank God for loving me. I ask him what he's got going today, because I would really like to be part of it.

Processing These Ideas about Prayer in Our Daily Lives

1. ***Write a Testimonial to Grace.*** Try to describe briefly the situation and the experience. Share this, if you can, with one other person. It is your personal "testimonial to grace."

2. *Write a Fifth Gospel.* The word *gospel* means "good news." In writing the Gospels, the first Christians were trying to share their good news with all generations to come. Write a gospel about you and your life. Entitle it "The Goodness of the Lord to Me." Even if you never share this faith story with others, your writing will help you become aware of God's gifts to you.

3. *Evaluate Your Relationship with God.* There are, for want of better words, "overdependent" and "underdependent" people. It is possible to be one or the other in our relationship with God. Some of us are overdependent. We constantly ask God to do things for us instead of asking God to enlighten us and to empower us to do those things. Others of us are underdependent. We proceed to make our plans and dream our own dreams. We are sure that we know what is best for us. Then we ask God to support our plans. We are upset when God does not give us what we are asking for. The ideal, of course, is to ask God to enlighten and empower us to know and to do whatever he has sent us into this world to do. Write an answer to this question: Do I tend to be overdependent or underdependent, or am I on balance in this matter?

I hope these thoughts on prayer, as well as all the other personal "beatitudes" presented in this book, will be helpful to you on your journey toward ever greater happiness. These pages have been my act of love for you. Thanks for your open mind and gentle hands. Remember me as loving you.

John Powell, S.J.